M000247601

DAVID R. ROSS was born in Glasgow
his life. He was convener of the Soci
fascinated by Scottish history from an
the moniker 'biker-historian' for his weekly column in their 'Scotland's Story' magazine supplement throughout the Millennium Year. His first book, *On the Trail of William Wallace,* was published in 1999 and entered the Scottish top 10 bestsellers list in its first week.

This success was followed by *On the Trail of Robert the Bruce, On the Trail of Bonnie Prince Charlie, A Passion For Scotland*, charting the burial places of the rulers of Scotland, and *Desire Lines,* a journey round lesser known places in Scotland. His next book, *For Freedom,* described Wallace's last month and the 700th anniversary commemorations. His 2008 book, *James the Good: The Black Douglas*, was based on new research he had undertaken.

Ross conveyed in his books his unashamed passion for Scotland's landscapes, traditions, history and future. Most of his spare time was spent travelling around historic sites, battlefields and castles. He worked hard to promote Scottish interests and inspire a hands-on approach to history, regularly appearing on the History Channel both in the UK and North America where he undertook many speaking tours. In 2005 he organised a long overdue 'funeral' for Wallace 700 years after his execution, preceded by the Walk for Wallace, in which David walked 450 miles from the spot in Robroyston where Wallace was captured in 1305 to his places of 'trial' and execution in London. His Walk for Wallace attracted worldwide media attention and culminated in a public march through central London, from Westminster Hall to St Bartholomew's Church for a memorial service a few yards from where Wallace was executed on 23 August 1305.

David died suddenly and unexpectedly on 2 January 2010 aged just 51. The David R. Ross Memorial Fund (www.davidrross.org) has been established to take his lifetime's work forward. A true friend of Scotland, his contribution will be apparent for generations to come.

A tremendous enthusiast for all things Scottish.
Alex Salmond, MSP, First Minister of Scotland

Scotland is my passion, its freedom my reason for being.
I'm lucky to get a chance to share that passion with others.
David R. Ross

By the same author:

On the Trail of William Wallace, Luath Press, 1999
On the Trail of Robert the Bruce, Luath Press, 1999
On the Trail of Bonnie Prince Charlie, Luath Press, 2000
Wallace & Bruce, Jarrold Heritage Series, 2001
A Passion for Scotland, Luath Press, 2002
Desire Lines: A Scottish Odyssey, Luath Press, 2004
For Freedom: The Last Days of William Wallace, Luath Press, 2005
On the Trail of Scotland's History, Luath Press, 2007
James the Good: The Black Douglas, Luath Press, 2008

Women of Scotland

DAVID R. ROSS

Luath Press Limited
EDINBURGH
www.luath.co.uk

First published 2010

ISBN: 978-1-906817-57-2

The paper used in this book is recyclable. It is made from low chlorine pulps produced in a low energy, low emissions manner from renewable forests.

Printed in the UK by Bell & Bain Ltd., Glasgow

Typeset in 11 point Sabon

Contents

Publisher's Foreword

DAVID R. ROSS first got in touch with Luath Press in 1998 at the prompting of historian Elspeth King, curator of the Stirling Smith Museum & Gallery, who had recently edited an edition of *Blind Harry's Wallace* for us. Somewhat diffidently, he showed me a manuscript, saying that, encouraged by Elspeth, he had had a stab at bringing together what he knew of his hero's life into a book. This we were delighted to publish as *On the Trail of William Wallace.*

David had an extraordinary, larger than life presence – at 6ft 5in he was certainly larger than most of us – and an unquenchable enthusiasm for Scottish history. *Women of Scotland*, his tenth book, was with us in manuscript form when we received the tragic news of his unexpected death. With the help of Fiona Watson – historian and curator of The Abbot House in Dunfermline – and David's daughter Kimberley, we have brought it to publication. David will be greatly missed but he certainly achieved a lifetime's ambition, in that he was a dedicated and effective populariser of Scotland's history. His books will continue that life's work into the future.

Gavin MacDougall
Luath Press

Behold, I see my Father, I see my Mother,
I see my Sisters and my Brothers,
I see the bloodline go back through the days of Bruce and Wallace
to the very first Scot.
They call to me, and one day I will join them in the land of Tir Na Nog
where the heroes and patriots of Scotland live forever!
David R. Ross 2009

(Adapted from the film *13th Warrior* and the 13th century Ibn Fadlãn manuscript.)

Preface

I HAVE WRITTEN quite a few books about Scottish history. Several of these have been biographies of characters from our past, and I have written about them in a populist and easily absorbed way. I read 'heavy duty' academic history books all the time to expand my knowledge, and I couple this with constantly exploring the Scottish countryside. There are plenty of academic books out there and I see little point in repeating someone else's sterling work, so I try to tell my tales more in the manner of a *seannachie*, a storyteller from the old days. I truly hope that my books come across as historical entertainment. I'm also especially keen on trying to get people to visit the sites I write of and get to know the landscape of this ancient nation of ours. There is so much to see and understand when following in the footsteps of the men and women who have gone before, those proud Scots who have stood up and been counted when this country was threatened in any way.

And there is the rub.

My books up to this point have all been about warriors, males who led men onto and on the field of battle. It's time I wrote something about the women of Scotland. After all, our oldest chronicles say that the very name of Scotland came from a woman – and though it may be legend, it's a story our school kids should all know, and they don't. I want to rectify that!

The women I write about in these pages are not always the ones you would expect to read about. For instance, there are so many good biographies about Mary Queen of Scots I don't see the need to add yet another recap of her life. It might appear somewhat random, but to be honest this selection represents my own personal choice of women's stories I wish to bring to a larger public.

So herein are gathered a few tales about the fairer sex of Scotland.

Often in my daily life I find that it is the women of Scotland that have the true patriot souls their menfolk sometimes lack. Scotland means something to so many of them, and Caledonia burns deep within their collective memory. I hope that both Scots men and women are inspired or moved by some of the stories told here.

Women of Scotland, it is you who will bear and nurture our future generations. Instil in them a pride in their blood that will inspire the generations yet to come, so that our land will regain its place, and remain strong and free, defiant and proud, for the Scots yet unborn.

David R. Ross

CHAPTER 1
Scota

IT MAKES SENSE when writing a book about Scottish women, to start with the very first Scottish woman mentioned in our early chronicles, even if she is only a legend from antiquity.

According to the Chronicles of John of Fordun started in the latter half of the 14th century after Edward I looted much of our documentation during his raids, we are told that the germination of the Scottish people began about 1,600 years before the birth of Christ. Back in those times there existed a man called Gaythelos. His origins are reported in various ways, most often that he was a son of Heolaus, King of Greece, and was extremely handsome – almost beautiful – in countenance. But he was also wayward in spirit and so his father would not allow him to wield any authority. Gaythelos rebelled and many spirited young men flocked to his side till he had what almost amounted to an army of his own, whereupon he was cast out of Greece by force and ended up in Egypt. It is said that he arrived there backed by an army and helped Pharaoh Chencres eject the Ethiopians who had invaded Egypt.

Interestingly, Chencres was on the throne of Egypt at the time of the parting of the Red Sea and was drowned when the waters rushed back into place, as described in the Bible.

No matter how he arrived in Egypt, we are told that Gaythelos fell in love and married the daughter of Chencres, a girl by the name of Scota. As the tales of St Brendan tell us: 'a certain warrior reigned over Athens in Greece; and that his son, Gaythelos by name, married the daughter of Pharaoh, king of Egypt, Scota, from whom the Scots derived their name.'

Gaythelos' followers, being a matriarchal people (a trait shared by many Celtic tribes), took on Scota's name. From this time on they called themselves the Scots. The reason these people took the matriarchal side is straightforward, and quite obvious when you think about it. There could be doubt about who the 'daddy' was in some relationships, but with a growing belly and then giving birth, there was not a lot of doubt about who 'mummy' was, and so her blood-line was paramount.

This band of warriors set out to the west to find a homeland, setting sail across the Mediterranean. They must have made landfall on many occasions on this journey, and it was from one of these stops that the first legends of the Stone of Destiny began.

The Stone is a potent talisman for the Scottish people. Her kings were crowned sitting on the Stone and many legends surround this mythical chair. It is said that wherever the Stone is found, from there the Scots shall be ruled. King Edward I of England, known by his nickname, 'Longshanks', looted the Stone from Scotland and had it taken south to Westminster Abbey. In time, the rule of Scotland went to Westminster. The loss of this precious artefact caused much unrest among the Scots and there was outrage that it was kept in English hands and used for English coronations.

The Stone was returned to Scotland in 1996 and taken to Edinburgh Castle where it is on display with the Scottish Crown Jewels, the oldest of their type in Europe. In 1997, only a year after its return, the Scots voted for a parliament of their own again – in Edinburgh. So the old legend surrounding the Stone – that wherever it sits, from there the Scots shall be ruled – has come to pass!

One of the names by which the Stone is known is Jacob's Pillow. You may know the story of Jacob from the Bible. He rested his head upon a stone, whereupon he had a dream of angels ascending and descending from Heaven. A legend has it that Jacob was one of the Scots tribe and that this incident took place as they sailed along the coasts of North Africa. When Jacob informed his companions of what had taken place, they decided that they would carry this Stone on with them... and the rest, as they say, is history.

Gaythelos, Scota and the rest of the Scots eventually settled for a while on the coast of Spain. Scota later bore a son, Hyber, and it is said that the old name for Ireland, Hibernia, comes from him (to pursue that would entail us getting into another line of legend altogether!).

Eventually the Scots wanted to escape from the constant warring with the local Spanish inhabitants and again set sail, travelling through

the Pillars of Hercules, now the straits of Gibraltar, and entering the western ocean to search for a homeland. They settled first in Ireland and some centuries later they crossed from the north of that island into Scotland to amalgamate with the Celtic people already settled there – the Picts – who had held off the might of the Roman Empire and forced them to build their great walls.

Some of this may seem a little far-fetched to modern sensibilities, but I do have to say that Gaelic is very close in root to Sanskrit, a language of the East. In fact, King James the VI of Scotland used to delight in telling his English courtiers that Gaelic was the language spoken in the Garden of Eden!

In the mid 15th century John of Fordun's chronicles of Scotland's story were continued by Walter Bower in the Scotichronicon; he wrote these 11 books in the abbey on the island of Inchcolm in the Firth of Forth.

There is a colour drawing of Scota wearing a long blue dress and a large, round hat, standing in the stern of a ship with her husband as they set sail from Egypt westwards to find their homeland. This drawing is in the copy of the Scotichronicon kept in Corpus Christi College, Cambridge. I have no idea why we do not have a copy of such an important part of Scottish history kept within Scotland. Perhaps this is something historians could look into, that an English institution should still have such an important part of our history in their keeping, especially when it was a book written to try and replace historical documentation stolen by an English king. Scottish historians should be demanding its return.

After some thought, I realised there was indeed a 'Scota' connection that can be visited in Scotland. In Dunfermline Abbey there is the 'Great West Window' designed by Sir Noel Paton, a famous Scottish painter who submitted an unused design for the National Wallace Monument on the Abbey Craig near Stirling. This window features four persons from our history: Malcolm Canmore; his wife, St Margaret of Scotland; King Robert the Bruce, our hero-king; and Sir William Wallace, champion of our people. Wallace stands, mighty sword in hand, over the crouching form of a blonde girl – a hero of Scotland standing guard over the spirit

of the people, in the shape of a maiden. This girl is a representation of Scota, the girl who gave our people their name.

I like to tell kids the story of Scota, and give the girls a wee edge of superiority. Their very nation is named after one of their own!

CHAPTER 2
Deirdre of the Sorrows

THE STORY OF DEIRDRE is reasonably well known in Ireland, yet almost unknown in Scotland. It is a tale that has been woven into Irish folklore, one of their great early legends, but the likelihood is that Deirdre was a Scot. By saying 'Scot', I mean that she was born in what we know today as Scotland, although the name would not yet be coined for many centuries. She was of Celtic stock, born at a time when there were strong ties between Scotland and Ireland with much travel on the sea routes between the lands. Her tale belongs to both sets of inhabitants.

There are several translations of her tragic story, mostly dealing with her early years in Ireland. The full implications of her name, Deirdre NicCruithnigh, should be explained. The appellation 'mac' used in Scottish names simply means 'son of' – for example, the name MacLeod means 'the son of Leod'. In this day and age English speakers generally use this masculine form. But in Gaelic culture a female is known as 'nic', meaning 'daughter of', as in NicLeod. This is an important point to make in a book about Scottish women.

Deirdre's second name is often mistranslated as 'daughter of the musician', from Cruitear, a musician or harpist. But Cruithnigh (pronounced Crew nee) is actually the name that the ancient people of her part of Scotland were known by. It is often written 'Cruithne' in modern text, but we know these people better as the Picts.

You might not know that as well as the moon, planet Earth actually has another natural satellite in orbit around – named Cruithne. Honestly, we have two moons! Though I have to say that Cruithne, discovered in 1986, is only five kilometres across and when it is close to the Earth it is still 30 times further away than the moon.

Nice that it has a Celtic name though!

Deirdre's name is quite literal in its translation. She was the daughter of the King of the Cruithne. A veritable princess. As often happened in those days, when Deirdre was still a young girl her father had her betrothed to a powerful man, people of that blood-stock to ensure strong ties. Her intended was Conchobar, the King of Ulster, who was to send for her when she became 18.

Deirdre spent her formative years in Glen Etive in the first century AD. The site of their home still survives. Dun MhicUisneachan, the fort of the sons of Uisneach, is sited at Ledaig on the Benderloch shore of outer Loch Etive. I am indebted to the late W.H. Murray, Scottish climber and writer who had an outstanding knowledge of the west Highlands, for the sites of some of the locations in the story of Deirdre.

And for the influence he had on me!

I read and re-read his *Companion Guide to the West Highlands of Scotland*, trying to learn every detail that a life dedicated to the subject had absorbed. It was through his work that I first heard of Deirdre.

In Glen Etive she developed a strong relationship with three brothers, the sons of Uisneach. All three loved her and she loved all three in return. She was closest to Naoise. The four lived a golden lifestyle, having adventures galore in the Etive hills. The boys would hunt for deer, fish or badger, and they would eat out in the open, often at what is now known as Deirdre's waterfall in Glen Etive. Her story mentions her fondness for a place called Tigh Grianach (House of the Sun). This probably stood on the slopes of An Grianan (1,795 feet), to the west of Kinlochetive. Another place-name in her story is that of Coille Naoise. Coille is the Gaelic word for 'wood' or 'woodland', so it simply means Naoise's Woods. These trees are at the back of the bay between Achnacloich and Airds Point.

The idyllic life of Deirdre and her friends came to an end on her 18th birthday. Conchobar had sent a party over to Scotland to take his intended bride to Ireland, but Deirdre could not bear to be parted from the sons of Uisneach, and no matter what her father or Conchobar said, she would not leave without them. Eventually, trying to find a compromise, Conchobar's representatives agreed that the boys should accompany her to Ireland.

Whilst on the ship, Deirdre composed a ballad, 'Farewell to Alba' (Alba is of course the ancient name that people used for the land and is still the Gaelic name for Scotland). It has survived the intervening centuries and has no doubt been changed over the years, but I am sure its essence is preserved. It covers that very human of desires, the love of one's homeland, and I'm sure its sentiments have been echoed by the many generations who have been forced to leave Scotland, for instance, during the Highland Clearances.

A lovable land is yon eastern land,
Alba, with its marvels,
I would not have come hither out of it
Had I not come with Naoise.

Lovable are Dun-fidga and Dun-finn,
Loveable the fortress over them,
Dear to the heart Inis Draigende,
And very dear is Dun Suibni.

Caill Cuan!
Unto which Ainle would wend, alas!
Short the time seemed to me,
With Naoise in the region of Alba.

Glenn Laid!
Often I slept there under the cliff,
Fish and venison and the fat of the badger,
Was my portion in Glenn Laid.

Glenn Masain!
Its garlic was tall, its branches white,
We slept a rocking sleep,
Over the grassy estuary of Masain.

Glen Etive!
Where my first house I raised.
Beauteous its wood, upon rising,
A cattle fold for the sun was Glen Etive.

Glen Da Ruad!
My love to every man who hath it as a heritage!
Sweet the cuckoos note on bending bough.
On the peak over Glen Da Ruad.

Beloved is Draigen.
Dear the white sand beneath its waves;
I would not have come from the east,
Had I not come with my beloved.

On landing in Ireland, Deirdre realised that she was unable to marry Conchobar, due to her love for the three boys with whom she had been raised. Conchobar, furious and feeling he had been cheated, had the boys put to death, at which Deirdre wrote the following lament:

The lions of the hill are gone,
And I am left alone, alone.
Dig the grave both wide and deep,
For I am sick and fain would sleep!

The falcons of the wood are flown,
And I am left alone, alone;
Dig the grave both deep and wide,
And let us slumber side by side.

Lay their spears and bucklers bright,
By the warriors side aright,
Many a day the three before me,
On their linked bucklers bore me.

Dig the grave both wide and deep,
Sick I am and fain would sleep,
Dig the grave both deep and wide,
And let us slumber side by side.

It is one of the great romantic stories of early Scottish literature and has been told among the Celtic people across two millennia. It is said that the Irish druids granted her last wish and she was indeed buried beside the sons of Uisneach as she so strongly desired.

Today, as you drive the little winding road down Glen Etive you are looking to the hills that Deirdre so loved. The view to the two Buachailles, the great herdsmen who stand guard over Glens Etive and Coe, their shapely crags towering on either side of the hill pass known as the Larig Gartain, is one of the most memorable in Scotland – and that is saying something. Deirdre's own home was said to be on the left side of the river where grassy slopes face Dalnain Lodge.

As a much younger man I scrambled over the hills of Glen Etive. I wish I had known then of the story of Deirdre; I could have enriched my experience with thoughts of times past, so many centuries ago, and those others who loved these hills and their call.

CHAPTER 3
Symbol Stones

THERE ARE STANDING STONES scattered over the length and breadth of Scotland. Some of these monoliths were put in place in the days when our earliest ancestors came to these shores. The later versions, dating from the 6th to the 9th centuries, are covered in carved symbols.

No one knows for sure what these symbols mean, but the fact that they are repeated on stones hundreds of miles apart shows the importance they had in their day. The symbols themselves have gained modern appellations to describe them. There are crescents with v-rods, double disks with z-rods, and many of the stones bear figures of armed men or animals.

Every animal depicted can be easily identified – a boar or a deer, a wolf or a snake – apart from one creature, which appears many, many times and seems to be from the realm of fantasy; it has become known as the 'Celtic beast'. It looks like a sea creature, as it has what look like flippers instead of feet, as well as a long crocodile-type snout. There is a tassel-like appendage emanating from the back of its head. It is not at all fearsome though – it has a cuddly, friendly look about it, or does to me at least!

This Celtic beast may be a representation of a 'kelpie', the water-horse who would trick the unwary to climb on its back and lead them to a watery grave. Or perhaps it depicts one of the creatures that inhabit our lochs, like 'Nessie' in Loch Ness or 'Morag' in Loch Morar.

I have realised on my travels that many of these stones stand in places where our old chronicles tell of the death of a king, or on the site of a battle of hoary antiquity, so the symbols most likely tell the story of the events that transpired there.

Many standing stones bear symbols that look like close representations of the 6th–9th century walrus ivory combs and bronze-backed mirrors which can be seen in such places as the Museum of Scotland in Edinburgh. It has been suggested that such symbols perhaps refer to places where queens or noblewomen may have had influence or been involved in events; or perhaps they mark the places where they died.

One of the most famous is the 'Maiden Stone', which gained its name from the mirror and comb symbols carved upon it. It is located near the tiny village of Chapel of Garioch and is signposted from the A96 – it stands a little south of this major route. Within the trees on the opposite side of the road from the Maiden Stone, there is a statue of 'the maiden' herself. Holding a mirror like the one depicted on the nearby stone, she is quite an overwhelming lady, a dozen feet tall. I have never been comfortable turning my back on her! I somehow feel that her sightless stone eyes open wide when I'm not looking.

Another female-orientated carved standing stone is Vanora's Stone, now in the little museum at Meigle in Perthshire which contains many fine examples of such ancient artistic work. This stone originally stood atop the mound in the graveyard outside the museum, but like the others in this collection it has been moved indoors to protect it from weather erosion. (I should point out here that some historians say that the motif on the front of Vanora's Stone actually depicts the Biblical Daniel in the lion's den.) Locally, this stone and the mound it originally stood above were believed to mark the last resting place of Vanora, a lady known more widely as Guinevere, the wife of the legendary King Arthur. Among the many other sites in Scotland that lay claim to be associated with Arthurian legend are Merlin's grave near Drummelzier on the River Tweed and Arthur's Seat, the craggy backdrop to Edinburgh city centre.

Perhaps one day Scotland will discover its own 'Rosetta Stone'– the stone that revealed the meaning of Egyptian hieroglyphs – and the true meaning of our symbol stones will be revealed. But in the interim the art of our ancestors is attraction enough. I love to locate these stones and gaze with wonder upon their beauty. You too can roam the landscape of Scotland and try some deciphering work of your own, and see if you agree with me that the mirrors and combs must surely be symbols relating to women.

CHAPTER 4
Gruoch – Lady Macbeth

DUE TO SHAKESPEARE'S famous play, Lady Macbeth is one of the best-known Scotswomen in the world. But it would be wrong to assume that she is a fictional character, as some of the characters undoubtedly are, Banquo for one.

Macbeth was King of Scots from 1040 till 1057. Gruoch, the basis for Lady Macbeth, was his wife and queen. We know very, very little about Gruoch's life and Macbeth is only mentioned in our chronicles something like three times. We do know that he reigned for 17 years, which was quite a long time for those days. Many of our royal figures were the victims of dynastic struggles, stabbed to death or poisoned so that one of their relatives could sit on the throne in their stead.

As for Gruoch, we do not even know her date of birth. She was the granddaughter of Boite, a son of Kenneth III of Scotland, so as great-granddaughter of a king, she had royal blood in her veins. We do not know the date of Gruoch's first marriage, but her husband Gille Coemgain mac Mail Brigti, who was Mormaer of Moray, (the term 'mormaer' being an earlier equivalent of 'earl)', was burnt to death with some 50 of his followers in 1032. He was survived by their son, Lulach, who later became a king of Scots.

This story has a really interesting twist. Gruoch's first husband with his 50 followers were most likely killed on the orders of Macbeth as an act of revenge for Gille Coemgain's murder of Macbeth's father in 1020, some dozen years before.

It may seem bizarre that Gruoch went on to marry Macbeth, her husband's murderer. Some say this could have been because she was regarded as a chattel and was forced into the marriage. But when Macbeth eventually became king she was known as queen in her own right and not just as a queen consort. The granddaughter of a King of Scots, it seems she was a lady of status and power and knew exactly what she wanted and was in charge of her own destiny.

Her actual character has been overtaken by the persona of

Shakespeare's Lady Macbeth and the blood-soaked shenanigans that she gets involved in. Shakespeare, literally, puts words in her mouth. The real personality of Gruoch is unknown.

The story of the dramatic Macbeth has become so embedded that various locations are pointed out as being the place where this or that event in the play took place. One such is the 'blasted heath' where Macbeth met the three witches. Near to Brodie Castle in Morayshire a sign points the way from the A96 trunk road, the mile and a quarter to 'Macbeth's Hillock'. This green mound is said to be the place where the 'weird sisters' foretold Macbeth's destiny.

Shakespeare may have based this incident on a story in Holinshed's Chronicle, written around 1587, where it is reported that Macbeth was confronted by women in 'strange and wild apparel', who hail him with prophesies before disappearing. Shakespeare's Macbeth was written sometime between 1603 and 1607 for the delectation of King James VI of Scotland, who inherited the throne of England in 1603. It can be seen as an exercise in diplomacy and flattery, an effort to win the king's patronage.

When the real Macbeth and Gruoch married, Macbeth adopted Lulach, her son from her first marriage. There is no record of the pair having had children of their own. One of the most extraordinary events of Macbeth's reign was the report by a monk based in Mainz in Germany, that in 1050 the king had made a pilgrimage to Rome, where he scattered 'silver like seed to the poor of the city'. This raises many interesting points.

Firstly, it gives the lie to the evil man that is portrayed in the Shakespeare play and in some chronicles, as the pilgrimage would have been carried out as an act of piety. Secondly, Macbeth must have had tight control over his kingdom, being able to leave it during such unruly and turbulent times in a state of relative peace and quiet for the long road to Rome, knowing that there would be stability in his absence. The fact that he scattered silver also shows that Scotland may not have been the poor cultural backwater many seem to assume. Thirdly, there is a good chance that Gruoch accompanied her husband on this trip to the Eternal City.

Imagine the city as Gruoch might have seen it. Rome was the first city on Earth to reach a population of over a million souls, roughly two thousand years ago. No other city would reach this level of population till London, in the early 1800s. But by the time of Macbeth's reign in Scotland the city was at its lowest ebb, with a population of perhaps 10–20,000. The Roman remains would have been very impressive, with the like of the Coliseum still fairly intact; an earthquake in the 1300s caused most of its ruin.

I'm sure Gruoch would have been fascinated travelling to a place where so many well-known deeds of history had taken place.

We have no date of Gruoch's death or knowledge of her place of burial, although when Macbeth was slain at Lumphanan in 1057 (not at Dunsinane as in the play) his body was eventually taken to the island of Iona, that sepulchre of royalty.

Only one charter has survived that bears Gruoch's name. She endowed land to the then holy men of Scotland, the Culdees as they were known. The Culdees built themselves a monastery on St Serf's Isle on Loch Leven, in Fife. (The scant remains of this priory should not be confused with Loch Leven Castle, which stands on a different isle on the loch.) St Serf's is a bird sanctuary today and is not normally accessible, but it is a lasting reminder of its benefactor, Gruoch, Queen of Scots.

CHAPTER 5
St Margaret

ST MARGARET OF SCOTLAND, or Margaret Atheling to give her pre-canonised name, is one of the most famous women in Scotland's past. She was born in Mecseknádasd in Hungary, where the ruins of Castle Reka are pointed out as the place of her birth (in the late 1040s), into a family of English royal blood. In fact, her grandfather was the ousted English king, Edmund Ironside.

After the death of Edward the Confessor, who had founded Westminster Abbey and was buried therein, Margaret's family were invited back to England with the view that her brother Edgar could contend for the crown, but in fact Harold became king. Then the Norman William the Conqueror invaded England in 1066 and defeated the English at the Battle of Hastings, where Harold was slain. England came under the control of foreigners and the ancient English line of royal blood came to an end.

Margaret's family sailed north into the realm of Scotland. Her ship landed at a little bay in the Firth of Forth that has since become known as St Margaret's Hope. Malcolm Ceannmor, King of Scots, was based not far from the north bank of the Forth, in his fortress at Dunfermline. Word was soon brought to him that Margaret and her company had landed and the Scots court hurried to greet them. Malcolm assured them that they were welcome in Scotland and could seek sanctuary there, or simply use it as a resting place before moving on.

On the journey to Dunfermline, Margaret, growing weary, rested upon an old carved stone that was probably once part of an old stone circle. She is said to have rested upon this stone often in the years that followed, on her journeys from Dunfermline to the Forth. This stone, which has over 80 ring markings, stood in its original location till 1856, when it was moved to an adjacent site to allow for road widening. It can be seen today, standing upright with a stone bench below, at the entrance to Pitreavie Business Park on the south side of Dunfermline. Among the legends which have grown up around it, one affirms that women who wish to become pregnant should sit on it for a while, as Margaret was wont to do!

After marrying Malcolm Ceannmor, Margaret moved into the royal residence. Dunfermline takes its name from this place: 'Dun' means a fortification, usually on a hilltop, and 'ferm-line' is a corruption of 'bend in a stream', so it basically translates as 'the hilltop fort in the bend of the stream'. This description suits the site of Malcolm's residence perfectly.

From the gate of Pittencrieff Park at the front of Dunfermline Abbey, signposts direct you to the place where Malcolm gave Margaret's party sanctuary. Only low walls now stand on the hilltop site of his royal residence. I suppose we should be thankful that at least something remains after the best part of a millennium.

Malcolm soon fell in love with Margaret and wished her for his queen. She had made up her mind that her life would be dedicated to God and had envisaged that she would perhaps become a nun, but it seems her family convinced her that marriage to Malcolm might be no bad thing and that she could use her influence to promote Christianity in Scotland.

The marriage took place in the little Celtic chapel that predated Dunfermline Abbey. Margaret became Queen of Scots aged about 24, Malcolm being 16 years her senior. The monarch rules over his or her people, but like the rest of us only has tenure of the land for one lifetime – so they are not rulers of Scots' land'. There is a story that not long into the marriage Malcolm began to have doubts about Margaret's fidelity, for she often disappeared on her own, no one knew where. One day he went after her. She went down to the stream that meandered round the castle and followed its course several hundred yards upstream. Malcolm watched as she entered a little cave hidden in the undergrowth and waited a few moments before going in behind her. He was surprised to find that she had set up a little altar there and was kneeling in prayer before it. Being a pious woman, she had looked for a little spot where she could contemplate in peace, a little like the early Christian missionaries in Scotland who had set themselves up monk's 'cells' where they could be alone with their thoughts.

Malcolm is said to have built Dunfermline Abbey, under Margaret's guidance, as somewhere she could express her religious devotion. But perhaps she preferred the little cave as a place to pray, looking for relative peace away from the courtiers who surrounded her.

The lovely thing is that Margaret's cave has survived all that the centuries have thrown at it. As time went on it became full of debris, but it was cleared out in 1877. The biggest threat to its existence came with the proposed development of a car park, but there was a public outcry and the cave was preserved.

In one corner of the Glen Bridge car park off Chambers Street there is a visitor centre inside a cottage-like building; 87 steps lead down to the cave, with storyboards telling of the life and influence of Margaret on the way down. In the centre of the cave there is a model of the praying figure of Margaret, clutching a cross. Admission is free. It is nice to be down there in the relative peace and quiet, standing where our saintly queen prayed over 900 years ago.

Dunfermline Abbey, impressive as it is, is a shadow of its magnificence in medieval times when three monarchs with their full retinues could have been accommodated in the building. It became a magnet for pilgrims and a ferry service over the Forth conveyed visitors there, hence North and South Queensferry, named after the little boats that once plied their way across the water. The Forth rail and road bridges now span the gap, with the rail bridge approximately following the line of the old ferry.

Margaret bore Malcolm eight children, six boys and two girls, all of whom survived to adulthood at a time when child mortality was high; given also Margaret's periodic fasting in the name of religion, their survival is extraordinary indeed for that day and age. Three of her boys in succession became Kings of Scots.

Margaret's life was spent modernising religion in Scotland. Although she did great and good works, she was also responsible for ousting the influence of the native Celtic Church. I have heard much debate on this over the years. Some see it as the start of the Anglicisation of Scottish culture, something that has always been to Scotland's detriment.

From a purely Scottish perspective, Margaret's life can be viewed from two different angles. She spent much of her time helping to create works of beauty to adorn Dunfermline Abbey, sometimes commissioning artisans from abroad to help in this work. One such item, a gospel book colourfully and beautifully crafted with capitals picked out in gold, became Margaret's most treasured possession. We will shortly come back to this gospel book.

We know so much about Margaret because her confessor, Turgot, wrote an account of her life only a decade after her death. He tells us how, every day, as queen, she would personally wait on a crowd of the poor and needy and feed them. Travelling the length and breadth of Scotland with her husband, she would scatter gifts to the ordinary people they passed at the roadside.

Interestingly, Turgot informs us that King Malcolm could speak fluent Latin, Gaelic and English, but unlike Margaret, he could neither read nor write. Turgot notes that he omits much detail of Margaret's life, purely because some of the miracles surrounding her were so extraordinary that people might have thought he was making them up!

Margaret brought a relic with her to Scotland, a relic that has imbued itself with an almost mythical status in our history books. She had in her possession a piece of wood that was said to be a piece of the True Cross on which Christ was crucified. In Scotland the old word for a cross was 'rood', so it became known as the Holy Rood. Her son who became David I had his own adventures with this relic, and in consequence founded Holy Rood Abbey at what is now the bottom end of Edinburgh's Royal Mile. Holyrood Palace was later built adjoining this abbey, and today Scotland's Parliament building is known as 'Holyrood'. All part of Margaret's continuing legacy.

An intriguing aside is the story that Arthur of the Britons had a piece of the True Cross that was handed down the generations to Margaret's grandfather, Edmund Ironside, who took it with him when he fled to Hungary (Margaret came from Hungary, of course). This nice wee legend links up very different eras of history.

Turgot does mention that Margaret had a heavily jewelled cross which she venerated, but whether this contained the piece of the True

Cross, or whether the Holy Rood was actually shaped like a cross, we have no way of knowing.

And what happened to the Holy Rood? Edward I of England looted it during his invasion of Scotland in 1296, when he took the Stone of Destiny and much of our documentation south. It was kept in London, but after the wars fought by Wallace and Bruce, England recognised Scotland's independence and signed the Treaty of Edinburgh in 1328. As part of the peace process, the Rood was returned to its rightful home at Holyrood Abbey.

Unfortunately the son of Robert the Bruce, David II, did not have his father's genius for warfare. He had the Rood carried with his army on an invasion of England. At the Battle of Neville's Cross, fought on 13 October 1346, near Durham, the Scots were soundly defeated. The English attributed the victory to the intercession of St Cuthbert, to whom Durham Cathedral was dedicated. The Holy Rood was placed upon the Shrine of St Cuthbert and the many captured banners of the Scots were placed round about it. The Rood remained at Durham Cathedral till the Reformation, when it disappeared, no one knows where.

Malcolm and Margaret died within a short period of time. In 1093, following the death of William the Conqueror, Malcolm decided to invade England continuing the turmoil in that country. Just a few months earlier he had journeyed south to lay the foundation stone of Durham Cathedral. We can see Margaret's influence behind this pious act, and I'm sure that the fact her blood was that of the royalty of England was a part of it too.

Malcolm besieged Alnwick Castle in Northumberland and the English garrison agreed to surrender. We are told that one of the garrison leaned forward to symbolically hand over the keys on a spear-point, and that as Malcolm reached for them, the Englishman thrust forward with the spear and stabbed him fatally in the eye. All accounts, both Scots and English, say that Malcolm was 'basely betrayed'. Some peasants found Malcolm's body and it was taken in a cart to Tynemouth Abbey, where he was buried in a makeshift tomb. Twenty years passed before he and Margaret would be reunited inside Dunfermline Abbey.

Their son Prince Edward had been wounded at Alnwick and had died near Jedburgh as he made his way back north.

Margaret, residing at Edinburgh Castle, was seized with acute stomach pains and was lying in agony when Edgar (another of her sons who had been at Alnwick with his father) came into her chamber. Seeing her distressed state he did not want to inform her of the events that had taken place, but Margaret told him that she already knew.

She called for the Holy Rood, and holding it above her, cried out, 'All praise to Thee, Almighty God, who hast been pleased that I should endure such deep sorrow at my departing, and I trust that by means of this suffering it is Thy pleasure that I should be cleansed from some of the stains of my sins.' Turgot recounts that as she exclaimed 'Deliver me!' the life left her body. The pallor of illness was replaced in death by warm hues, which he takes as proof that she had entered the Kingdom of Heaven.

Margaret's body was wrapped in a shroud, but enemies of Malcolm and Margaret were already gathering to besiege Edinburgh Castle with a view to seizing the throne. Her retainers were worried about how they would transport her safely to her beloved Dunfermline. Luckily, a haar came in from the Firth of Forth and they were able to spirit her body from the castle to the Queen's ferry, to be conveyed across the water. It has been claimed that a higher source was responsible for this miraculous mist appearing at such an opportune time.

On the highest point of Edinburgh Castle rock stands the city's oldest surviving building, the tiny, but rightly famous, St Margaret's Chapel. The original use of this structure had been long forgotten by the early 1800s, when it was used as a powder store. In 1845 it was realised that there were the features of an early religious establishment within this rectangular edifice less than 30 feet long, but it was not until 16 March 1934 that it was rededicated as a chapel. Although it is quite a plain place, it has a certain air about it.

I vividly remember being taken there as a boy, hearing some of Margaret's story and seeing the copy of her Gospel Book under glass, and the carved Norman archway. It struck a chord within me then, though it would be many years before my country's history came to mean something more tangible deep within my soul.

Some time after Margaret's death, steps were taken to have her elevated to sainthood. One of the stipulations of canonisation is to have proof of miracles taking place around the person concerned. One of those that the Scots reported was that Margaret's body had not decayed. Another concerned her illuminated Gospel Book. Turgot tells the story of how it was being transported across Scotland by a carter, possibly following Margaret and Malcolm as they held court across the country. As the driver negotiated a river, it fell into the swiftly moving water. It was only when the carter reached his destination that the loss was discovered and courtiers set out to search his route. Eventually the handwritten, hand-coloured gospel book was discovered and fished out of the water. To everyone's surprise it was found to be intact – none of the writing had washed off, the illuminated letters shone in their original glory and the only damage was a few damp patches on the final pages. The book was returned to Margaret and she valued it even more highly, believing that God had protected it from harm.

The Gospel Book 'resurfaced' again eight centuries later. In 1887 an item described in an auctioneer's catalogue as an 'English work of the 11th century' was put up for sale by an individual who hailed from Bristol. A poem written in Latin on the flyleaf describes how a king and holy queen once owned the book and recounts Turgot's story of Margaret's Gospel Book. The damp marks on the final pages settled its identity. The Bodleian Library, the main research library at the University of Oxford, bought it for six pounds. Thus an item of such huge historical significance to the people of Scotland came to be kept in England.

A people are the result of their history and what is subtracted from this history is subtracted from the people too.

Margaret was canonised in 1250 and a shrine was built to contain her remains, situated hard against the east end of Dunfermline Abbey. It is said that when her original burying place was opened, the church was filled by fragrant odours emanating from her tomb. The bearers lifted her coffin to convey it to her new resting place. As they passed the spot where Malcolm was buried, the coffin became so heavy that they had to drop it to the floor. Extra hands rushed to help, but no matter how they tried, the coffin could not be lifted. Someone suggested that Malcolm's coffin be lifted too – and when it was borne aloft, it was found that Margaret's coffin could then be lifted. They were carried together to Margaret's new shrine.

St Margaret's shrine at Dunfermline became a magnet for pilgrims, visitors from the south using the ferry across the Forth originally set up by the patron. The shrine was beautifully decorated. It resembled a small church in form, and Margaret's coffin was enclosed in a wood cover inset with gold and precious stones, which could be lifted to reveal the holy remains within. Her 'shirt' was also kept at Dunfermline as a holy relic. (This shirt was present when Mary of Gueldres gave birth to the future James III, and was there when Margaret, Queen of James IV, gave birth to the future James V.)

Although this might seem bizarre to modern sensibilities, Margaret's head, still with its strawberry-blond hair, was taken to Edinburgh Castle for the birth of James VI, son of Mary Queen of Scots. The cult of Margaret seems to have a special connection to all things connected with pregnancy and childbirth.

Margaret's relics and shrine survived unscathed till the Reformation in Scotland in the 1600s, where there was huge upheaval when the Protestant Church replaced the Catholic, and anything that smacked of 'idolatry' was smashed by mobs fired up by their preachers. Dunfermline Abbey suffered terribly, with the tombs of the many kings buried over the centuries destroyed – what a terrible waste, to destroy such beautiful art in the name of God.

To protect what he could, the last abbot of Dunfermline took the remains to his house at Craigluscar. The 'hows' and 'whys' are somewhat sketchy, but the remains seem then to have been taken to Spain, where the King, Philip II, liked to surround himself with holy remains and artefacts; it is reported that he spent much time stroking such objects. The remains are still at the Escorial, his palace just outside Madrid.

A Jesuit priest took Margaret's head, kept in a reliquary – a special bejewelled and ornate case – to Antwerp in 1597, where it was put on display for veneration. In 1627 it was taken over the border to the Scots College in Douai in northern France, where it remained until the French Revolution in the late 18th century, when the college was sacked and the head disappeared. The historian Carruthers reported that the head was in a state of 'extraordinary preservation, with a quantity of hair, fair in colour, still upon it'.

Standing outside Dunfermline Abbey today, I can look a few miles southeast to the Forth bridges marking the route of the old ferry, and beyond Edinburgh see the Pentland Hills, their outline the same as when Margaret looked upon them. The Great West Window of the abbey contains a panel depicting Margaret, and one depicting Malcolm stands alongside. Just a short hop away from the abbey is the Town House of Dunfermline. The Kirkgate front has four busts as part of its ornamentation; these busts are of Malcolm, Margaret, Robert the Bruce, and his wife Elizabeth. The low walls and base of Margaret's shrine can be seen at the east end of the abbey grounds. The plinth that contained the coffins of Margaret and Malcolm sits in mute testament to those past days when pilgrims travelled to affirm their faith.

CHAPTER 6
Queen Ermengarde

ERMENGARDE WAS NOT SCOTTISH. It was an adopted land for her, but she became queen consort and is buried in Scotland. Her father was a vassal of Henry II of England, Richard, Vicomte (viscount) of Beaumont-sur-Sarthe in France, and she was a granddaughter on the 'wrong side of the blanket' of Henry I of England. Born in 1170, she was named after the Merovingian Ermengarde, from whom she was supposedly descended. The Merovingians were the first dynasty of the kingdom of the Franks, their name coming from Merovech, a fighter who battled at the time of the decline of the Roman Empire. Their first real king was Clovis I, who was baptised at Reims with 3,000 of his followers in 496 AD, and so became the first barbarian king to take the Catholic faith. The Merovingian dynasty lasted four centuries, the original Ermengarde marrying Giselbert, who reigned from 846 till 863 AD.

King John of England recommended 'our' Ermengarde as a wife to William I of Scotland; they were married on 5 September 1186, at Woodstock Palace in the town of Woodstock, Oxfordshire.

Our history books know William I of Scotland as William the Lion, not so much from his martial ability as from the fact that he adopted the Lion Rampant as the Royal Standard of Scotland. Before his time, a Pictish boar had been the king's banner. The story goes that William was presented with a pair of lions as a gift, perhaps brought to this country from the Crusades. (There is part of Stirling Castle known as 'the Lion's Den'.) William liked his lions so much that he wanted one to be depicted on his personal standard. His personal standard-bearer would fly this banner on the battlefield, marking his position in those days of heraldic devices, so it was the war banner of the King of Scots too. As a lion standing on its back legs clawing is known in heraldry as 'rampant', Scots generally call this flag by its familiar name 'the Lion Rampant'. It is a lion depicted in red on either a yellow or gold background.

It seems William was a robust character. To the Gaelic-speakers of Scotland he was known as Uilleum Garbh, which translates as rough, or brawny William. Even the portraits on his coinage show him uncrowned and tough looking, muscular and unshaven. He was not so lucky that his personal strength helped him in his wars against England however. At one point William was captured by the 'Auld Enemy' and England began to assume that Scotland was some sort of sub-kingdom.

William was born in 1143, so he was 27 years older than Ermengarde when they married. She bore him four children: Margaret in 1193; Isabella in 1195; Alexander, who would inherit the throne as Alexander II, in 1198; and Marjorie in 1200.

On his death in 1214, William was buried at the high altar of the magnificent abbey he had built at Arbroath. This abbey would play a prominent part in the future history of the Kingdom of Scotland, being the place where the Declaration of Arbroath was ratified in 1320. That magnificent document has spoken to us over the centuries, proclaiming Scotland's independence from interference by others and telling of our rights as a sovereign people.

Arbroath Abbey was founded in 1178, dedicated to the Virgin Mary and Thomas à Becket. Becket, who had been martyred at Canterbury Cathedral only seven years before, was said to be a personal friend of William. Either that, or William based his dedication on the fact that Becket had humbled the King of England, and was therefore a fitting man to commemorate!

William's tomb, rediscovered in 1816, was constructed of hewn freestone. An effigy in the abbey is reputed to be of William, but it may be of one of the abbots of Arbroath. A modern grave slab now marks his burial place at the site of the high altar.

A few years ago I was in Arbroath for the commemoration of the Declaration of 1320 and a few of us went to the abbey for a visit. We stood at the tomb of William the Lion, unfurled a Lion Rampant, and took a few photos. Irate members of staff approached us and said that they could not allow us to take photos where a Lion Rampant was present as it was considered to be 'political'. We tried to explain that we were at the tomb of the King of Scots who actually 'invented' that flag and it was in honour of that fact that we were taking pictures. They did not see it that way, insisting that any such gestures were of a political nature. I still fail to understand how displaying a flag pertinent to Scotland, therefore an apolitical gesture, can be seen as an affront in any way. Unionism, I'm afraid, with all the elements of the Scottish cringe that that unnatural credo brings.

William died in Stirling on 4 December 1214 and was borne across Scotland to his final resting place, leaving Ermengarde a widow at the age of 44. Their third child replaced William on the throne. As mother of Alexander II, Ermengarde would have occupied a position of respect and could have 'relaxed', but it seems she did not rest on her laurels for the rest of her days. In 1227 she founded a new religious establishment at Balmerino on the south side of the Firth of Tay. Balmerino stands some three and a half miles southwest of Dundee by water, and a little over seven miles northwest of Cupar. She brought some Cistercian monks from Melrose to take over the running of the place. Balmerino village served as a port. The abbey afforded views up the Tay towards Strathearn, and the airy hilltop site was regarded as being a healthy location. The abbey, second pointed in style and measuring 240 by 140 feet, was parted by eight octagonal piers into two parallel aisles. Scant ruins of the transept, the sacristy and the chapter house survive, mostly fenced off to protect visitors from injury from the crumbling stonework. It is no wonder that the abbey is in such a ruinous state. It was burnt by the English in 1548 and then suffered at the hands of a mob fired up by reforming religious zeal in 1559.

Nearby buildings have obviously benefited from the abbey's stonework in the intervening centuries, with recycled masonry apparent in their construction. One farm has a complete window with decorated surround lifted entirely from the site, with what looks like a piscina (a stone bowl for holy water, the word coming from the same root as Pisces) set above.

I recall seeing a roadside sign on the drive down towards the ruins which stated: 'Beware! Free Range Children'. That made me smile.

Ermengarde died on 11 February 1233 and was buried at the high altar of her abbey at Balmerino. Although that part of the original church has vanished, a large stone cross marks her last resting place. I thought it a little strange that she was not laid to rest beside her husband in Arbroath Abbey, as that was standard practice in those days, just as it is now. It may suggest that there was a distance between them as a couple, or it could simply be that William was buried in the abbey he founded and loved. And when Ermengarde's time came, she perhaps wanted to be buried in the little abbey that she so loved, in the rolling farmland overlooking the Tay.

One can go to these ruins and think of a girl, a descendent of the Merovingian dynasty of France, of the blood-line of the English kings and queen consort of Scotland. She is buried far from her ancestors, but her little abbey was a legacy that she left on the landscape of Scotland, and her blood mixed with our royal line.

CHAPTER 7
Devorgilla

DEVORGILLA IS A FAMILIAR NAME to anyone who studies Scottish history. Most books dedicated to the Scottish Wars of Independence usually mention her in the first few chapters, as she was the mother of King John Balliol. She is particularly well known in the southwest, the area of Scotland she called home. Her legacy of building in stone has ensured her survival in the memory of the hardy people of Dumfries and Galloway.

We are not entirely sure of her date of birth, but an educated guess puts it in the year 1210. She was one of the children of Alan, the Lord of Galloway. Galloway was very much part of Celtic Scotland, the people being Gaelic speakers at that time. In fact, the name Galloway derives from *Gall-Gael*, basically meaning 'foreigner Gaels', as that is what the population of Galloway was to the Gaels who inhabited the western seaboard and islands of Scotland.

Devorgilla's name would seem to be from the Gaelic *dearbhfhorghaill*, which translates as 'Daughter of the Oath'. She came from a distinguished line: her grandfather, David I of Scotland, was also the Earl of Huntingdon in England. He was a younger brother of two Kings of Scots, William the Lion and Malcolm IV, that latter often known as 'Malcolm the Maiden' due to the fact that he became king at a tender age and was unmarried. Devorgilla steps into our history books in 1223, at the age of 13, when she married John Balliol, an important English nobleman whose many lands were ruled from Barnard Castle in North Yorkshire. The impressive remains of this castle still stand in the town of the same name, which lies a little to the north of the A65 Penrith to Scotch Corner route. To be married at such a young age was not an unusual occurrence in those days, especially among the gentry. But Devorgilla seems to have fallen deeply in love with John. It is believed that he was born in 1208, which would have made him about 15 at the time of their marriage. Together they became very wealthy, much of this wealth emanating from the extensive lands that Devorgilla brought to their union. John had lands in both England and France, the Balliols having come over to England during the Norman Conquest, from their ancestral lands of Bailleul near the Somme, where the earthworks of their castle can be seen in woodland near the village of Bailleul, about 10 miles from Abbeville.

Devorgilla would bear John eight children; the fourth, named after his father, became King John I of Scotland, who ruled from 1292 to 1296 (Edward I said he was no longer king in 1296, and we don't want to believe him!). John's elder siblings had all predeceased him and died childless. He got into a serious dispute with the Bishop of Durham, so incurring the displeasure of the King of England; by way of compensation, in 1263, he provided funds for scholars to attend a 'college for the poor' at Oxford University. He died in 1268. Devorgilla established a permanent foundation at Oxford in 1282 and set up a code of statutes that is still, loosely at least, used today: this is the famous Balliol College, and its main historical society is the 'Devorgilla Society'. Devorgilla seems to have been devastated at her husband's death. Before he was buried, his heart was removed and placed within an ivory casket bound with silver. Devorgilla took this casket everywhere with her for the rest of her life. At meal-times she would often have food served before this casket, almost as if John was present at the table. The food would later be given to someone poor or needy.

On 10 April 1273 Devorgilla signed a charter to establish a new Cistercian abbey on the west bank of the River Nith, some six miles south of Dumfries. The spot chosen was a beautiful one, nestling in a tree-covered landscape under Criffel Hill. This attractive building constructed of rose coloured sandstone became known as 'New Abbey'. One of the reasons for this moniker came from the fact that an older establishment, Dundrennan Abbey, stood by the Solway Firth some 30 miles by road further to the southwest, near Kirkcudbright. The name 'New Abbey' survives in the name of the village that surrounds the abbey ruins today. Devorgilla was responsible for the founding of many religious establishments, but it is this one that stands out as her crowning glory.

When she died on 28 January 1289 at Kempston in Bedfordshire, her body was brought the long journey north to New Abbey to be buried in an impressive tomb at the high altar, the ornate case containing her husband's heart clasped to her breast.

As time passed, due to Devorgilla's style of burial with her treasured memento of her marriage, people began to call the 'new abbey' Dulce Cor, Latin for Sweet Heart. It is by this name that the abbey is known today.

Sweetheart Abbey suffered badly at the time of the Reformation, but it is still well worth a visit. It is a veritable jewel of a place. Centuries ago it fell into disuse, and locals used it as a convenient quarry. But in a strange twist, in 1779, locals united in helping to preserve what was left of it so that it could serve as an 'ornament' to the locality. And ornament it is. Its ruined, rose-coloured walls and main tower look attractive at any angle, and still dominate the village. Pieces of the later effigy of Devorgilla have been collected and rebuilt with modern, sympathetic stonework to replace what was missing. The building is only a shell of its former glory, but there are other things to look out for once you have paid your respects to its founder.

At the entrance to the graveyard there is a memorial to William Patterson, a local boy who became the man behind the Darien Scheme, Scotland's bid to become a trading power in the 1690s. One of his other claims to fame was that he was the founder of the Bank of England and the Bank of Scotland. Something else to look out for is the remains of the abbey precinct walls, of which there are large sections at the far side of the car park and the graveyard. They are constructed of irregular blocks, some big enough to make you wonder how they were raised into place. When you look at them, you think of the days when monks wandered this enclosure. The mill in the village is built on the site of the original, which was operated by the monks.

Most visitors to Sweetheart Abbey and the grave of Devorgilla will travel through the town of Dumfries en route. 'Devorgilla's Bridge' over the River Nith is a stunning example of medieval architecture. Constructed in the same rose-coloured stone as Sweetheart Abbey, it has breakwaters projecting from each of its piers. A few of the arches at the eastern, town-centre end are missing, which gives it a slightly truncated look. But, it is still a joy to walk across, as so many Scots have done in centuries gone by. Devorgilla financed the building of the first bridge over the Nith in 1280. It seems the existing bridge replaced it in 1431. It could be that it was only partially reconstructed and much of what is on display is actually Devorgilla's original, or contains much of the original stonework. No matter, it is a link with many preceding centuries of Scottish history, and it has withstood all the floods and torrents that the Nith could throw at it over the years. A little downstream from Devorgilla's Bridge is a weir, 'the Caul', which crosses the river at a slight angle, and at one time the water it diverted turned the waterwheels of mills.

At the turn of the millennium, artworks depicting Devorgilla were constructed at either end of the Caul: the one on the east bank made of stone, its counterpart on the west bank, of glass. Unfortunately the latter was so badly vandalised in 2008 that it had to be removed. It was flat like a mirror, and was indeed like a mirror-image of Devorgilla, looking across to her stone counterpart. This part of the artwork represented Devorgilla emerging from the water of the Nith. I hope that it will one day be replaced and that local youth will begin to take a pride in their history in this changing Scotland, and show such works the respect they deserve.

A later chapter of this book is devoted to Margaret, Maid of Norway, the little girl who was the rightful Queen of Scots but who died before she was able to ascend to the throne. Devorgilla died some eight months before the Maid, at what must have been about 80 years of age, impressive longevity for those times. If she had outlived the Maid, she would have been the next in line to the throne of Scotland. Devorgilla would then have been the first queen 'regnant' that Scotland had ever had.

CHAPTER 8
Marjorie, Countess of Carrick

MARJORIE, THE WHOLLY Celtic Countess of Carrick, was born sometime prior to 1256. Probably best known for being the mother of King Robert the Bruce, she seems to have been a strong-willed, fiery woman. A remarkable story regarding her marriage to King Robert's father has come down to us.

Her first husband was Adam de Kilconquhar. In the late 1260s, when Marjorie was probably in her late teens, he went off to fight in the eighth crusade. One of his companions was Robert Bruce, the sixth Lord of Annandale. Adam was killed at Acre in the Holy Land and on his return to Scotland, Bruce travelled to the seat of the Countess of Carrick at Turnberry Castle in Ayrshire to tell her the news. It seems Marjorie was very taken with this handsome young man. It is said that she held him captive at Turnberry until he agreed to marry her. No shrinking violet was Marjorie.

Turnberry Castle is a ruin, but enough remains to give us an idea of the size and style of the place. A cave runs from the sea into the heart of the castle, which would have been a handy means of supplying the place if it was under siege. A lighthouse stands in the midst of the ruins today, and it is surrounded by the world famous Turnberry Golf Course. There is an access road running across the course to the lighthouse, so you can park and walk to the castle remains. As it is the most likely birthplace of King Robert the Bruce, and the site is very picturesque, looking out to the Ailsa Craig, Arran and Kintyre beyond, there are several reasons to visit.

Robert Bruce, Lord of Annandale, eventually agreed to wed Marjorie. The fact that he would become Earl of Carrick by right of his new wife may have had some bearing on his decision, but perhaps I am being unkind. Maybe he was seduced by the charms of the young countess. Certainly the fact that two leading personages of the realm of Scotland became husband and wife without the blessing of King Alexander III upset that monarch, who took steps to punish them, as

John of Fordun recounts in his chronicle of the Scottish nation, 1363, as given in Skene's translation of 1872:

> the common belief of the whole country was that she had seized – by force, as it were – this youth for her husband. But when this came to King Alexander's ears, he took the castle of Turnberry, and made all her other lands and possessions be acknowledged as in his hands; because she had wedded with Robert of Bruce without having consulted his royal majesty. By means of the prayers of friends, however, and by a certain sum of money agreed upon, this Robert gained the King's goodwill, and the whole domain.

It seems that things were smoothed over, and that theirs was a very happy union indeed, producing at least nine children. Isobel, the eldest, born in 1273, went on to marry King Eric of Norway. The future King Robert was born on 11 July 1274, most likely at Turnberry Castle, as that was his mother's house and I would imagine that that is where she would want to be in such circumstances; there have been wild claims that Robert was born in Essex and that he was not really a Scot. Brix is the root of the family name 'Bruce'; although his forebears came over from Brix, near Cherbourg, in France in 1066 during the Norman Conquest of England, his father's side had been in Scotland for seven generations, and as already mentioned, his mother was of old Celtic stock, of the line of Carrick. I find it hard to believe that he did not think of himself as a Scot through and through. Certainly the English chroniclers have no doubt about this, referring to Bruce's fight against English rule as having taken place because he 'was a Scot born in Scotland'.

Local legend says that he was baptised at Kirkoswald, and there is an ancient font in the now ruined church that is pointed out as being the one used. Kirkoswald, only a few miles inland from Turnberry, was the local parish church, so Marjorie would have been familiar with the place.

Marjorie, Countess of Carrick, died in 1292. Her burial place is not recorded, although there are several possibilities – Kirkoswald being a main contender. Her husband lived on till 1304. He is buried in the church of Holm Cultram in Cumbria. This building was badly damaged in an arson attack in June 2006. His carven tombstone has survived; it stands upright in the porch of the church. By strange coincidence, also interred in this church are the brain and entrails of Edward I of England, who died at Burgh-by-Sands in Cumbria and he was embalmed before the journey south to Westminster Abbey.

Before he became king, Robert the Bruce used the title he inherited from his mother and he is commonly known in documents of the period as 'Earl of Carrick'. His daughter from his first marriage to Isobel of Mar was called Marjorie, after his mother.

CHAPTER 9

Margaret Crawfurd of Corsbie

MARGARET'S MAIN CLAIM to fame is that she is the mother of the great Scottish patriot, Sir William Wallace. The only mention of her is to be found in the work of Blind Harry, a wandering minstrel who told, then wrote of the deeds of Wallace in the 1400s, more than a century after Wallace's cruel murder in London in 1305. That is not to say that Harry was wrong in his identification of the lady who gave birth to our patriot son, but he does get Wallace's father's first name wrong! Harry names him as Malcolm Wallace, but examination of Wallace's seal on the famous Lübeck Letter gives us 'William filius Alan' – Latin for William son of Alan. Corsbie was an estate in the vicinity of Ardrossan. Assuming Margaret was William's mother, she married Alan Wallace and moved into the Wallace family home at Elderslie near Paisley in Renfrewshire. The family also had land not far distant from Elderslie, at Auchenbothie near Howwood. There has been the usual Scottish arguing about where the location of Elderslie was, as there is a house with a similar name in Ayrshire, but as this house was not built till about 1850 and Wallace was born around 1270, I think we can safely put these arguments to rest! The Wallace family were vassals, men in the service of the Stewart family, the High Stewards of Scotland, who lived in nearby Renfrew and parcelled out land to their followers, including the Wallaces.

Harry tells us that Margaret firstly bore Alan Wallace a son named Malcolm. This is certainly correct, as we know from other sources that William had an older brother by this name. Perhaps Blind Harry thought that the oldest boy was named after his father and that is how the mistake in Margaret's husband's first name arose. William was the second son and there was a third named John. All three were patriots who fought hard for Scotland, but William's name is the one that has survived the centuries. There is the mention of a sister or two, but unfortunately we do not even have a record of what these girls' names might have been, never mind any details of their lives.

It seems William and his mother were close and that she very much approved of the life he chose, that of the good fight for his nation's freedom in the face of a tyrannical oppressor.

Langtoft's Chronicle tells us that after some trouble with the invader in Dundee, William and Margaret travelled along the Tay and crossed by ferry to Lindores on the south shore. Assuming the guise of pilgrims visiting the shrine of St Margaret, they then took the path now known as Wallace's road over the Ochil Hills to Dunfermline. It's funny to sit in the remains of St Margaret's shrine in the grounds of Dunfermline Abbey and think that Wallace and his mother might have sat on these same stone seats, looking at the last resting place of a king and canonised queen of Scotland. I'm sure Wallace thought of the long history of Scotland and how he could do his best for her future, without realising that he himself would one day be writ large across the pages of her story. They spent one night in Dunfermline then travelled on south via the Queen's Ferry to Linlithgow. Interestingly, Blind Harry tells this self-same story in his poem:

For at Dundee they call a justice eyre,
No longer then durst Wallace sojourn there,
His mother clad herself in pilgrim's weed,
Then him disguised, and both marched off with speed,
Nought to defend himself he had from foes,
But a small sword he bore below his clothes,
Away they went, none with them living moe,
When challenged said 'to St Margaret's we go'.

Close by Lindores, the ferry o'er they passed,
Then through the Ochils marched very fast,
Into Dunfermline lodged all that night,
And on the morrow, by day was light...

Exactly as it has it in Langtoft's Chronicle, they travelled on to Linlithgow. According to Harry, Wallace did return to Dunfermline to hide out in the woods there. The woods in question are most likely the ones that have survived in the vicinity of Pittencrieff Glen, not too far from the remains of the castle of Malcolm Canmore and within sight of the towers of Dunfermline Abbey. A little well covered by an iron grating by the Glen Burn in Pittencrieff that is still pointed out as 'Wallace's Well' is located on the side of the burn below the ruins of the royal palace of Dunfermline. It can take a little finding as there is not a path at that side of the burn and it is surrounded by undergrowth. I have wondered if it gained its name from the visits that Wallace had here during his sojourns.

Tradition tells us that Margaret predeceased her son by two years, in 1303. At least she lived to see his victory at Stirling Bridge in 1297, saw him knighted the following winter at the Kirk of the Forest in Selkirk and become Guardian of Scotland. It must be extraordinary to see your offspring become the leader of your country and I'm sure Margaret must have been very proud. It is widely held that she was buried at Dunfermline Abbey. In *The Picture of Scotland* (1827), Robert Chambers states that:

> In the churchyard there stood till 1784, when it was blown down by a tempest, a thorn tree of vast size and great apparent age, which was said by tradition to mark the grave of Wallace's mother. How that lady came to die here, is not known; but the tradition that this was her burial place is positive and general. It is added, that on burying his mother here, the Scottish patriot desired to erect a monument to her memory, but had not time, being obliged to remove his quarters, either in pursuit of, or in flight from his English enemies. As a next best, he planted this thorn, which continued to commemorate the event till its destruction, time and cause above-mentioned; when it was replaced by a stem from the old tree, which has reached a considerable size, and promises to continue the memory of Wallace's filial affection unto all time.

This tree has again been replaced, and the current one I have seen thrive on my many visits to Dunfermline Abbey over the last 20 years or so stands on a little mound not far from the gateway that leads to the

Abbot House. It is said that this mound is the site of the town's Weeping Cross, and that it was in this vicinity that Margaret was buried.

During medieval times, persons of standing were usually buried within the walls of the actual church. This practice continued up till the Reformation in Scotland, when it was then discouraged and people were buried in the surrounding graveyards. I would imagine that Margaret was a person of enough note to have been buried within, but I suppose that Wallace was perhaps too well-known a figure fighting against the occupying English to be seen to have been involved in such a project. It would have been simple enough to have had persons bury his mother and plant a tree, and he could have visited it in the graveyard without eliciting too much attention.

The date of Margaret's death is reported as being early in 1303. Perhaps it was just as well that, if buried at Dunfermline, she was not buried within the walls of the abbey. King Edward of England used it for his accommodation later that year and on marching his men away had the place set on fire, an unbelievable act of badness and evil. Most of the tombs were destroyed and the treasures of the place lost for future generations of Scots. It becomes even more ugly an act, if that is possible, when we realise that Edward's own sister was buried within. She had been married to King Alexander III of Scotland and had predeceased him; both were buried in an ornate tomb in Dunfermline Abbey.

To be honest, whether Margaret is buried at Dunfermline or not does not really matter. It is probably a question that will never be answered, so who can deny that it may be the truth? The fact that people believe it to be true, and visit the thorn tree (identified by a plaque) to leave flowers in memory of the mother of Wallace, is enough in itself. I'm sure from there they walk into the abbey and visit the grave of Robert the Bruce, and at least are also visiting the scene of the last resting places of many of Scotland's most famous names, even if there are no physical remains of their original tombs.

While here, make time to go into the garden of the Abbot House; on a side-wall, there is an exquisite plaque in memory of Margaret by artist Tim Chalk. It features her holding Wallace's younger brother John, the young William Wallace is depicted carving a wooden sword, the thorn tree and the abbey itself in the background. I love this plaque very much. It is made of bronze and so has taken on that greeny, aged effect, although it was only put in place in the mid-1990s. In depicting the Wallace family as real people and not just the folk of heroic legend, it conveys great pathos. It bears the legend: 'Margaret, mother of William Wallace, lies buried beneath a thorn tree in the grounds of Dunfermline Abbey'.

CHAPTER 10

Margaret, Maid of Norway

ON 12 MARCH 1286, Alexander III, King of Scots, was found dead near the water's edge at Pettycur Bay in Fife. Just a few months before, at the age of 44, he had married his second wife, Yolande, daughter of the Count of Dreux. Alexander had spent the day at a meeting in Edinburgh Castle; Yolande was on the opposite side of the Firth of Forth at Kinghorn in Fife. Although the weather was deteriorating, nothing would do for Alexander but to cross the stormy water and spend the time with his 23-year-old French bride.

When the ferry landed at the north shore, Alexander, a superb horseman, galloped off, leaving his bodyguard behind in the dark. When the bodyguard reached the castle at Kinghorn, the porters told them, nonplussed, that the King was not there. Kinghorn Castle, situated on rising ground to the north of the town, dated back to the 1100s and was a royal residence from the time of King William the Lion. Not a trace of it remains today.

At first light the bodyguard set off to retrace their route. They found Alexander, his neck broken. It seems that in the dark his horse had lost its footing and thrown the king over a cliff. Alexander was buried in Dunfermline Abbey. His tomb was destroyed at the time of the Reformation in Scotland.

The stone cross raised to mark the spot where his body was found was replaced in 1886 with an inscribed pillar surmounted with a cross. This pillar stands at a lay-by on the south side of the A92 coast road between Burntisland and Kinghorn. On the north side of the road there are high cliffs. I have attended commemorations here, celebrating the life of Alexander, who reigned well over Scotland. Much coinage of his reign has survived, showing how prosperous Scotland was under his guidance. He had seen off the threat of invasion by the Vikings, having defeated them at the Battle of Largs in 1263. Future generations raised in the shadow of war with England would remember his reign as a 'golden age'.

Although Alexander was gone, Yolande was pregnant and it seemed that the succession of Scotland might yet be assured. But when the time for her confinement came, the child was stillborn. Yolande, queen-regnant, left Scotland shortly after. She would later marry the Duke of Brittany and bear him six children. She died in France in 1330.

Yolande was Alexander's second wife. He had married Margaret, daughter of Henry III of England in 1251. She was the sister of the future Edward I of England – 'Longshanks' – who did all in his power in his later years to destroy Scotland.

Margaret bore Alexander III three children and things must have looked rosy indeed for the future of the Scottish monarchy. These children were: Margaret, b. 1260, Alexander, b. 1263, and David b. 1272. Alexander died in Lindores aged 20, David in Stirling Castle at the tender age of nine. Both brothers were buried in Dunfermline Abbey. Margaret survived to marry King Eirik II of Norway. She bore him a daughter, a little girl who is known to our history books as 'the Maid of Norway'. But ill luck seemed to follow the heirs of Alexander, and Margaret died while giving birth to this little girl at Tonsberg on the west side of Oslofjord. Margaret was buried in a wall tomb in the cathedral at Bergen; the cathedral was demolished in 1531 and today the site is marked by a memorial in the Bergenhus Fortress.

With Alexander's death without issue, his granddaughter, the little Maid, now became the heir to the throne of Scotland. She had been born in 1283, most likely at the beginning of April, so when her grandfather went over that cliff in Fife, she would be approaching her fourth birthday.

Alexander's one-time brother-in-law Edward, now King of England, involved himself in this child's future. He negotiated with her father Eirik, and even went as far as equipping a large ship at Yarmouth in England, filled with the confectionery of the day, to sail to Norway and bring the Maid to England. Eirik, to his credit, and referring to his daughter as 'Queen of Scots', sent the ship back to England without its intended passenger.

Edward's interest in the future of the Maid eventually led to a meeting between Scots and English delegates at Birgham on the River Tweed, on the Scots side of the border. Here a marriage between the Maid and Edward's son and heir, the future Edward II, was agreed to, the Scots being careful to add riders so that Scotland's independence was not compromised in any way. The treaty was signed on 18 July 1290. If this marriage had taken place it could have resulted in Scotland losing her sovereignty to England, the larger and more populous nation. The greater always seems to absorb the lesser in such matters. The Maid was also of the blood royal of Norway and so it could even have resulted in three nations having one single monarch. But these are speculations only.

Birgham today, a tiny village comprising a few hundred yards of houses straddling the road between Kelso and Coldstream, seems an unlikely place for such important negotiations to have taken place. Perhaps it contained some substantial buildings in those days, or it might be that a tented encampment was where the great lords of both countries stayed during these talks. Meanwhile, plans were already under way in Norway for the Maid to sail to her new kingdom with her retinue.

There is an old song, still reasonably well known in Scotland, by the name of 'The Ballad of Patrick Spens'. It is thought that it may be based on the fetching of the Maid home to her kingdom, intermingled with the fact that several Norse women married Scots royalty over the years. It begins:

> The king sits in Dunfermline town,
> Drinking the blude-red wine;
> O whar will I get a steely skipper,
> To sail this new ship o' mine?
> ...
> Our king has written a braid letter,
> And sealed it with his hand;
> And sent it to Sir Patrick Spens,
> Who was walking on the strand.
>
> To Noroway, to Noroway,
> To Noroway o'er the faem;

The king's daughter o' Noroway,
'Tis thou must bring her hame.

Interestingly, one of the later verses shows how close Norway was in terms of travelling time by sailing ship. Norway was not a country that seemed remote to the Scots:

They hoysed their sails on Monenday morn,
Wi' a the speed they may;
They hae landed in Noroway,
Upon a Wodensday.

Documentation surviving from that time tells us that two of the Scots knights who accompanied the Maid on her journey were Sir David Wemyss from Fife and Sir Michael Scott of Balwearie. The Wemyss family still have in their keeping a silver tray that is supposed to be a relic of this mission.

But poor Margaret – the bad luck that had beset former generations of her family cast its shadow over her, and she died in Orkney in October 1290. It is believed that her captain decided to make shore at Orkney because she was suffering from some sort of sickness, perhaps severe seasickness, though some sort of food poisoning or disease may have been the cause; one report says that 15 of the sailors on board either died or became seriously ill. The Maid died in the arms of Bishop Narve of Bergen. She was only eight years old.

Meanwhile her reception committee of Scots lords were waiting at Skelbo Castle at Loch Fleet, north of Dornoch in Sutherland. This castle is first mentioned in our records in the year 1211. It stands in ruins today, but there are substantial remains as it was inhabited up to the Jacobite period. Some of the outer walls and the remnants of a tower may date from the period of the Maid.

I have sat against the castle walls on a beautiful summer's day, looking over Loch Fleet, the tide out, the seals making the most of the exposed sandbars, and I've tried to cast my mind back to that day in 1290 when a lone ship sailed into the loch, bringing the dire news that the Maid was dead. Queen in name, but never to rule over her kingdom. At first the people of Scotland did not want to believe she was dead. Rumours abounded that she had recovered and all was well. But it was not to be.

The Maid's body was taken back to Bergen, where King Eirik demanded that her coffin should be opened so that he could examine her body, which he then ordered to be taken to the cathedral in Bergen, where she was interred in the tomb beside her mother.

Bergen Cathedral was destroyed during the religious upheavals in Norway's equivalent of the Reformation in Scotland. Although the building has gone, a memorial marks the spot where it stood. It has a plaque naming the royalty who were once crowned within the cathedral on one side, and on the other a plaque naming the people of royal blood buried there, the last two names being '1263 Dronning Margareta Alexandersdatter' and '1290 Jomfru Margareta Eiriksdatter'. ('Jomfru' literally means 'virgin' in Norse; from this appellation comes the Scots name for Margaret – 'the Maid'.)

There is a strange postscript to this story, as reported in the Iceland annals. In 1300 a woman from Lübeck in Germany, accompanied by her husband, appeared at the Norwegian court. She claimed that she was the Maid. She said that she had not died in Orkney; that instead, she had been sold by certain Norwegian nobles and raised in Germany. Her father had died the year before, which may be one of the reasons for this sudden appearance of the 'False Maid', given that Eirik had ordered the Maid's coffin to be opened and had been satisfied that it contained his daughter. Eirik's brother, Hakon V, was now on the throne. As the Maid had been born in 1283, this woman, if truly the Maid, would still only have been a teenager, but reports say that her hair was greying and she looked to be aged around 40. Strangely, some members of the court and several Norwegian churchmen seem to have believed her story and much debate ensued as to the validity of her claims.

King Hakon, who would of course remember his niece well, came to question this woman personally. with the outcome that she was declared an impostor, convicted of fraud, and burnt at the stake at Nordness; her husband was beheaded. But there were some who still believed her story. A church named Margaretaskirk founded near the spot where she suffered became a place of pilgrimage. Although there was some outcry at this, the church managed to survive till the Protestant Reformation swept through Norway, when it was demolished.

It would seem that prominent members of the Norse community coerced this woman into playing the part of the Maid for some political reason unknown to us. It seems strange that even though she was far too advanced in years to be the real Margaret, some were quick to affirm that she was indeed the Maid.

If she had survived, the Maid would have been the first female monarch to reign in Scotland in her own right. Her death would open the door for Edward I of England to begin his struggle to annex Scotland to his realm of England, using the state of flux in a leaderless country to try and exert his will. If she had survived, perhaps we would never have had our great national hero William Wallace come to the fore, and Robert the Bruce would have been accorded a mere mention in our history books. As she boarded the ship to take her to Scotland, I'm sure this poor little girl would never have realised the impact, albeit posthumously, that she would have on the future of her country.

CHAPTER 11
Marion Braidfute

SIR WILLIAM WALLACE is one of Scotland's great national heroes. He was there for his country when an aggressive and bullying neighbour threatened its very existence. He rallied the ordinary people of Scotland and turned them into a unified force after Edward I of England had taken his armies over the length and breadth of Scotland, trying hard to obliterate the very name of our nation. Along with his co-commander, Andrew Murray, Wallace defeated the English at the Battle of Stirling Bridge in 1297.

The hard fact is that we know very little detail of William Wallace other than the main events of his life. We do not know his date of birth; we know nothing of his growing from childhood into adulthood. He strides fully grown onto the pages of our history books when he murders William de Hesilrig, the English Sheriff of Lanark, and ignites the flame of revolt against the usurpers of his land. He gathers an army and defeats the English at Stirling Bridge. He invades England and on his return is knighted at the Kirk of the Forest in Selkirk and, in the absence of a reigning monarch, is made 'Guardian of Scotland'. English Edward, outraged, brings another army north and defeats Wallace at Falkirk in 1298. After Falkirk, Wallace resigns the Guardianship, fights a guerrilla war and then travels to France and Rome to argue Scotland's case abroad. Following his return, the English shamefully betray and capture him at Robroyston near Glasgow in August 1305. He is then taken to London where he is hideously executed: Wallace is tortured and disembowelled at Smithfield, his atoms scattered to the four points of the compass.

For the more minor details of Wallace's life we must turn to folk tales, in particular the work of 'Blind Harry'. Harry, a minstrel in Scotland in the 1400s, wandered lordly establishments telling tales of Wallace. Luckily, these tales were written down and eventually released as a book, *The Deeds of Wallace of Elderslie*, which has sold consistently in Scotland since Harry's time. In fact, it is the second biggest selling book of all time in Scotland, only being outsold by the Bible. It was used as the basis for the screenplay of the motion picture *Braveheart*.

And what was it that prompted Wallace to rise up against the invader? What was the last straw for this young man? What was it that finally spurred him to risk all for his country? According to Blind Harry, it was the murder of his sweetheart that tipped Wallace over the brink.

Hesilrig's death at Wallace's hand is fact. Harry tells how Wallace fell in love with a girl he spotted at church in Lanark, and how they married there. The church in question must have been St Kentigern's, which served Lanark in the time of Wallace. Its ruins stand in the graveyard adjacent to the roundabout on the Hyndford Road, at the 'top' end of the town. You can walk the ruins and imagine the hero of Scotland and his sweetheart spending time together here.

Harry does not mention her by name; in a 1722 edition translated by Hamilton of Gilbertfield, she is referred to as 'Miranda'. It is possible that Hamilton is using the name in the archaic sense, Wallace's 'Miranda' meaning Wallace's poetic sweetheart.

Gilbertfield, an 'L' plan fortified tower house, still stands, albeit in a ruined state, near Cambuslang on the outskirts of Glasgow.

Tradition has always averred that 'Miranda' was in reality Marion Braidfute, heiress to her family's estate around Lamington tower, the ruins of which can be seen surrounded by trees in the shadow of Tinto Hill, between Lamington village and the River Clyde, not far from the M74 motorway.

As a child Marion would have played on the banks of the river which winds its way through gorgeous rolling hillside and woodland scenery. She came from a wealthy family. Apart from their lands in the Lamington area, they had a town house in the nearby 'big town' of Lanark. It was while she was residing there that she went to the church service in St Kentigern's and fate brought Wallace under her spell and changed the course of Scotland's history. (Their story is depicted in the movie *Braveheart*, in which Marion goes by the name 'Murron', the Scottish 'pet name' for Marion.)

Wallace was by this time making a name for himself as a patriot, but still seems to have been able to visit Marion in reasonable anonymity, in those days before 'Wanted' posters or photo-fits! On one visit, as he walked down the middle of Lanark's High Street, his huge stature attracted the attention of some members of the English garrison. They started to shout jibes, which he returned with good humour. But one Englishman went too far. Believe it or not, local legend tells us what was actually shouted to change the mood.

It is reported, and I have heard this from several different sources as: 'While you were away the priest has been calling to have a f**k at your wife!' In an instant Wallace reached for the mighty two-handed sword he wore on his back. It came round in a sweep and severed the forearm of the Englishman who fell back in a welter of blood, screaming in fear and pain. Soon other members of the occupying garrison ran to see what was afoot.

Marion, who had been watching for Wallace from a window and had seen what happened, ran to the front door and flung it open. Wallace, seeing his chance, sprinted for the door. Marion slammed it at his back. He was able to run through the house, across the back garden, through the back gate and out into open country. In those days, house fronts faced the streets and had strong back-garden walls which served as a continuous defence, like a town wall.

There is a 'Wallace's Cave' by the River Clyde, a mile or so from the town. Perhaps Wallace retired to this cave to see what way the wind would blow after his escapade. I'm sure that he never realised that the English would take vengeance on Marion to tempt him into the open, and to warn other Scots who were the masters. Knowing Wallace's devotion and single-mindedness, if he had any inkling of what was to befall her he would have taken Marion with him, or fought to the death to protect her.

The English Sheriff of Lanark, Hesilrig, when he heard the news of what had happened, descended on the scene. He had Marion brought out from her home and, according to Harry, ran her through with his falchion (a type of broadsword).

The spot where this terrible deed took place is still pointed out. A memorial stone marks the site of Marion's family town house. This stone was replaced in 2005, on the 700th anniversary of Wallace's murder by the English. The new memorial features Wallace holding Marion by the hands; they are face to face, he gazing down at her. The original drawing was made by my friend Andy Hillhouse, who drew the cover pictures for my books *For Freedom* and *James the Good: The Black Douglas*. Andy seems to be able to catch the 'spirit' of Scottish history in his art, and I'm proud to be able to get sneak previews of his work, and even prouder when he asks for my help in getting a scene just right!

This plaque is just to the left of St Nicholas Church, at the bottom of the High Street, at the entrance to Castle Gate. Marion would have been slain somewhere just in front of this church. There is a bell in St Nicholas said to be the oldest in Europe; it was cast in the 1100s and so Wallace and Marion would have been familiar with its knell.

I appeared in a television programme on the US History Channel in late 2005 to talk about the times of Wallace. To capture an overview of Lanark, the programme makers had permission to film from the steeple of St Nicholas.

I took the opportunity to climb up beside the old bell and I gave it a knock with my hand, just to hear a little ring. Such a simple wee thing to do, but for me it was a link across the centuries.

Young men of the town would have taken word of Marion's death to Wallace and we can imagine how great was his agony and wrath. He must have berated himself for unwittingly leaving her to her fate. One thing was for sure: Hesilrig must die.

Gathering like-minded young men to his side, Wallace stormed the castle. We are told that Hesilrig, having been alerted, rose from his bed and as he went down the stairs came face to face with Wallace, coming to seek him out.

Hesilrig is said to have asked who Wallace was and what was the meaning of this outrage.

He received the simple reply: 'I am Wallace! Die, Hesilrig!'

Hesilrig was cut down on the spot and Marion avenged.

This incident was the catalyst for a general rising in Scotland.

As word spread of what had transpired in Lanark, Scots determined to throw off English plans for conquest gathered to Wallace's banner till he had what amounted to a rag-tag army.

The rest, as they say, is history.

The site of the castle where Wallace cut down Hesilrig in revenge is now the location of the bowling green at Castlebank Park. Strange to stand on a summer's day, watching a quiet game of bowls, knowing of the bloody act that once transpired here. Earthworks still visible show that this site was once heavily fortified, standing as it does on a hilltop position.

Incidentally, the name William de Hesilrig means William 'of' Hesilrig; Hesilrig today is Hazelrigg in Chatton, not far from Heaton in north Northumberland, England.

So where was Marion buried?

I'm sure she would have been taken back to her family lands to be buried with her ancestors. In Lamington village the church stands in a circular graveyard – ancient graveyards like this are generally laid out on the line of old druid sites, perhaps a stone circle, perhaps a temple. When the Christian religion came to Scotland, churches were often built on these sites. The Christians absorbed many of the pagan practises that the people knew and were used to, Christmas and Easter being two festivals based on ancient ones. So these places were 're-used', partly to oust the old ways, partly because the people were used to worshipping on these spots.

I have one right outside my back door!

How old is the current Lamington Church? That is very much open to conjecture. After visiting it, Robert Burns composed a scathing verse about the coldness of the sermon and the coldness of the place itself. But the Norman Archway of a much earlier building still stands in a side-wall, partially buried, and filled in. It is in use as a war memorial, but of course the attraction is to imagine Wallace and Marion walking through this archway when they were at service whilst visiting her family home.

So Marion, if she is the flesh-and-blood reality of the wife of Wallace, would, I imagine, be buried somewhere in the confines of this circular area. Perhaps she was buried within the earlier church itself, as before the Reformation in Scotland in the 1500s, persons of note were usually interred within family vaults, most often beneath the floor.

Legends have multiplied around Marion and her legacy over the intervening centuries. One is that she and Wallace had a daughter who survived them both and grew up to marry William Baillie of Hoprig. That family has since claimed descent from Wallace. The Baillies certainly inherited Lamington in 1368, Sir William Hoprig being granted the charter of Lamington, but there is no concrete proof that there was any Wallace connection.

In Balnagowan Castle, near Tain in Ross-shire, there is a huge and ancient chair that is pointed out as being the 'chair of William Wallace'. As I am a Ross and Balnagowan is the seat of my clan, I asked for and was given access to see this mighty chair constructed crudely from large logs. It originally came from Lamington Tower. And so the Wallace connection has again been made, the story going that when Wallace was visiting Marion at the family castle, one as mighty as he must have used such a chair.

No matter the validity of much that has been told, Wallace did slay Hesilrig that spring day in Lanark in 1297. It was read out as a charge at his sham trial in London's Westminster Hall before his shameful execution at Smithfield in August 1305. Perhaps his love for Marion was the catalyst that led to his stunning victory at Stirling Bridge.

A little of Marion's life can be followed if you wish to make the connection, by visiting the plaque that marks her house in Lanark, and the nearby scene of her murder. The ruins of St Kentigern's, where she and Wallace met and were married, are at the top of the town. From there you can follow the course of the River Clyde upstream a dozen or so miles, and see the ruined remains of a later version of her family home in trees near Lamington Mains farm, not far distant from the little church where she may be buried.

I was there at night once, when an unusual phenomenon caught my eye. I thought it was a searchlight beam at first, bright and white across the sky. But then I noticed it arched and curved in a way that light couldn't. A storm was approaching and the other half of the sky was lit by the clear light of a full moon. I was seeing... not a rainbow

– no, a *moon*-bow. Instead of it being created with sunlight, it was the bright moon that was giving it light and instead of coloured stripes it was banded from white to grey. I stood and watched it with my companions.

On the walk back to the car, we met others gazing skyward. This extraordinary sight has lent an extra layer to my memories of Lamington and the stories of the girl that the hero of Scotland loved so deeply.

CHAPTER 12
The Bruce Women

I HAVE LONG HAD A FASCINATION with the fate that befell the women closest to King Robert the Bruce. I first read their story when I was in my mid-teens and since then I have tried to learn as much as possible, especially by visiting places associated with them and just absorbing what I could. There are five women in question here: King Robert's second wife and queen, Elizabeth de Burgh; Marjorie Bruce, his daughter from his first marriage to Isabella, a daughter of the Earl of Mar; Isabella herself, who unfortunately died after a few years of marriage, perhaps in childbirth; two of King Robert's sisters, Christian and Mary; and Isobel, Countess of Buchan. These women suffered terribly because of their association with Robert, and I wish to tell their story.

Robert had been involved in the Scottish patriotic struggle, but acceded to the peace of King Edward 'Longshanks' of England in 1302. It has long been thought that one of the reasons for this submission was his desire for the hand in marriage of Elizabeth, daughter of Richard de Burgh, Earl of Ulster, friend and companion-in-arms of Edward. Robert and Elizabeth were married at some point in 1302.

A few months after the judicial murder of Sir William Wallace in London in August 1305, Bruce got embroiled in an argument with John Comyn, his rival for the Scottish throne, in the monastery of the Grey Friars in Dumfries. In the ensuing fracas Comyn was stabbed to death. Robert knew that he had to take drastic action and be crowned King of Scots. He was inaugurated on 25 March 1306 at Scone, the traditional crowning place of the Scots' monarchy. Edward had looted the Stone of Scone, sometimes known as the Stone of Destiny, some 10 years before and it was now in Westminster Abbey in London, but the Moot Hill where the Stone traditionally sat was still there. Bruce was most likely crowned atop this hill, with other ceremonies taking place in nearby Scone Abbey. Scone Abbey was destroyed at the Reformation, but its site is in the vicinity of the little graveyard by the old cross of Scone a little to the northwest of the Moot Hill.

Elizabeth would also have gone through some sort of inauguration ceremony to install her as queen. It is reported (albeit by a hostile English chronicler) that she turned to her husband and said, 'Alas, we are but king and queen of the May', referring to the fact that she knew Edward of England would not be long in using all his powers to destroy her, her husband and all of Scotland, if he could.

Two long-established parts of the ceremony to install a King of Scots involved the monarch being seated on the legendary Stone of Destiny, the crowning stone that some believed to be Jacob's Pillow, the stone, the Bible tells us, where Jacob had his dream of the angels ascending and descending from heaven. (The stone was returned to Scotland in 1996. The old legends that state wherever the Stone sits, that is the place from where the Scots shall be ruled and this came to pass when the Scots voted to have a parliament of their own in 1997 and power started to be transferred to Edinburgh, where the Stone resides.)

The other traditional ceremonial rite was that the monarch be crowned by the Earl of Fife, who, as the premier earl of Scotland, ceremonially lowered the circlet of gold onto the new king's head. Duncan, Earl of Fife was 16 years old and unfortunately he was completely in the power of English Edward. But his aunt, Isobel, Countess of Buchan (who was most likely in her late 30s) knew where her patriotic duty lay. She rode to Scone from her family lands near Leuchars in Fife to represent her family and crown the new king.

English chroniclers wrote that Isobel crowned Robert because of her desire to be his mistress, but I have seen these accusations from English chroniclers right through our history, directed at women who did their patriotic duty. We can take that accusation with a pinch of salt, it being an easy way to sully the lady's reputation.

King Robert's daughter from his first marriage, Marjorie, and his sisters Christian and Mary would obviously have been present at his inauguration, along with other family members and a throng of supporters, both secular and clergy.

Elizabeth was right in her fears that Edward would not rest on his laurels when it came to taking action against what he saw as Scottish 'rebels'. By 5 April he had appointed Aymer de Valence as his lieutenant in Scotland and had given him permission to 'raise dragon', meaning English armies could unfurl the dragon banner and the rules of warfare, scant as they were in those days, could be utterly ignored. Carnage took place on a horrific scale. Some of Scotland's leading churchmen were captured and taken south in chains.

In June Bruce, with quite an extensive army, came to the walls of the city of Perth and invited de Valence to come out and fight. The King of Scots had made the mistake of thinking that the English would abide by the rules of chivalry, but the English saw the Scots as subservient to them, and the rule-book did not enter into the equation as far as they were concerned. De Valence said that he might fight on the next day, so Bruce, taking him at his word, headed a little west to camp in the broken woodland around Methven Castle. (A later version of Methven Castle still stands, painted white and therefore discernable at quite a distance, showing us the spot where the encounter took place.)

Bruce's men had discarded their armour and weapons and were resting, cooking or foraging, when de Valence and his army suddenly burst through the trees and the slaughter began. Bruce and his womenfolk, who had been with him since his inauguration and were in the camp, were soon surrounded by a group of Scots warriors and managed to fight their way out of the trap. They then headed west to the edge of the Highlands and made their way past Inchaffray Abbey. Scant ruins are all that are left of this once important establishment. From there they followed the track at the side of Loch Earn, up Glen Ogle, and dropped into the glens of the head streams of the River Tay at Loch Dochart, where a castle stood on one of its islets.

As they made their way up Strathfillan, which lies between Crianlarich and Tyndrum, they were waylaid and attacked again, this time by a party of MacDougalls who did not want Bruce as their king. Bruce's men did all they could to defend the womenfolk and fought furiously. When three MacDougall clansmen assailed King Robert himself, this master of the battleaxe used it to devastating effect, dispatching two of his attackers; the third fell back, still clutching the large Celtic brooch from the king's cloak. This brooch has survived and has come to be known as the 'Brooch of Lorne'. The spot where this fight took place is in the vicinity of the farm of Dail Righ, meaning the 'King's Field' in Gaelic, a reference to the events that took place here.

On the opposite side of the River Fillan, by the West Highland Way, there are the ruins of the little chapel from whence the strath takes its name. St Fillan was the holy man who brought Christianity to this part of the Highlands. (The root of the word strath means a wide glen with a river flowing through it.) Tradition tells us that Bruce was here, and it was perhaps at this building he made the decision to send his womenfolk away, hoping that they would not be exposed to the danger that he knew his presence would bring.

Before Bruce and his band took to the hills, ready to live off the land and fight a campaign, the ladies were given an escort which included the king's brother Neil, the elderly Earl of Atholl, and all the horses of the party. This group set off northeast, across the lands of Atholl, over the hills of Braemar and on to the sanctuary of the strong castle of Kildrummy in Aberdeenshire. It has been supposed that they were heading for the safety of the Orkney Isles, or perhaps they intended to go on to Norway, where Bruce's sister Isobel was dowager queen.

They reached Kildrummy, but enjoyed only brief respite from the attentions of the invader. The English got word that they had arrived there, and Aymer de Valence and the future Edward II of England sent forces against them. A traitor within the gates set the castle's store of corn on fire and the garrison was forced to yield. The ladies managed to escape. Perhaps they fled as the English approached and before a siege began. (Kildrummy Castle is an imposing ruin, standing picturesque in hilly surroundings, and is well worth a visit.)

On reaching Tain in Ross-shire, aware that the Earl of Ross was no friend of Bruce, the ladies took sanctuary in the little chapel of St Duthac's. But the Earl violated that sanctuary and had the ladies seized and sent south as prisoners to King Edward.

St Duthac's Chapel today is a ruin standing in the centre of Tain's cemetery, another place to visit and cast one's mind back to the days of the Wars of Independence. As a Ross, I am of course embarrassed by the pro-English stance taken by the earl on this occasion. But I'm glad to say that the family were soon to see the error of their ways, for the earl's son, Sir Hugh Ross fought bravely against the English at Bannockburn in 1314.

Edward I was famous for his outbursts of temper. The English often remember him as a strong monarch, whose traits suited his role. But his ferocity against the nations he sought to conquer has left a legacy of hate against his name. It was his aim to try and terrorise the Scots into submission by using torture and murder. Many were the horrific killings in the second half of Bruce's inauguration year of 1306. The poor old Earl of Atholl, captured escorting the ladies, was hung from an especially high gallows and his body subsequently decapitated and burnt. Neil Bruce, the king's brother, likewise captured at Tain, was drawn, hung and beheaded at Berwick upon Tweed. Fifteen of Bruce's most loyal knights were hung at Newcastle upon Tyne on 4 August.

Sir Christopher Seaton, King Robert's brother-in-law, who had been present when the stabbing of John Comyn took place, was captured at Loch Doon Castle, south of Dalmellington in Ayrshire. The castle, which now stands on the lochside, was moved from its original position on an islet out on the loch and rebuilt stone by stone when the loch level was raised in 1935 for hydroelectric purposes. The castle is 11-sided, built in this fashion to fit closely the contours of the islet.

Sir Christopher Seaton was much loved by the people of Scotland. He was a chivalrous and dashing knight, a fitting match for the king's sister. So much was he admired that the people nicknamed him Sir Crystal. All this chivalry notwithstanding, on King Edward's instructions he was taken to Dumfries to suffer a hideous death. He was drawn, hung and beheaded on an eminence in the town that became known as 'the Crystal Mount'.

In later life Christian Bruce raised a little chapel here, dedicated to the Holy Rood, in memory of her much loved husband. St Mary's Church crowns this mound today; to the right, at the top of the stairs leading up to the church, there is a little fragment of Christian's original building, placed here by Major James Adair in 1840, and I'd like to say thanks to the major for his farsightedness in saving a little bit of history for future generations. Even today, the church newspaper is called the *Crystal Chronicle*.

News of the capture of Bruce's womenfolk was brought to King Edward. Torture and death followers of Bruce had come to expect, but in those chivalric days, ladies, especially those of 'breeding', might hope to be treated with courtly conduct. Because of this, King Edward's instructions as to the fate of these women seem particularly brutal.

Edward was not always savage to women, or at least he did not behave like a beast towards those who were not of Scottish blood. When his beloved wife, Eleanor of Castille, died in 1290 near Lincoln, it took 12 days for her coffin to reach Westminster Abbey in London. At each spot where her body rested, Edward had an ornate stone cross erected in commemoration. The three that have survived are known as 'Eleanor Crosses'.

Two of Bruce's women 'got off lightly' in comparison to the others. Queen Elizabeth was to be confined in a manor house at Burstwick in Holderness, the little peninsula that forms the curving north shore of the estuary of the River Humber; she was allowed two elderly women companions, chosen because of their stern demeanour. Elizabeth was after all, the daughter of King Edward's old companion in arms the Earl of Ulster. Christian Bruce, now widow of Sir Christopher Seaton, was confined in the Gilbertine Nunnery at Sixhills in Lincolnshire.

King Robert's other sister, Mary, was treated in a much harsher manner, reportedly because she had made derogatory remarks regarding King Edward. She was confined in a strongly latticed cage of timber and iron and hung over the walls of Roxburgh Castle, like an animal in a zoo, for all to gaze upon. Isobel, Countess of Buchan, who had committed the terrible 'crime' of crowning Robert, was encased in a similar cage hung over the walls of Berwick Castle.

These two women were to spend several years in this humiliating confinement.

Even more shocking was Edward's treatment of King Robert's young daughter Marjorie, who of course had no influence on events, being only 11 or 12 years of age and whose only crime was to be Bruce's blood relation. He ordered that she be confined in a similar cage in the Tower of London and allowed to talk to absolutely no one. Even his close advisors were aghast and thankfully he was persuaded to revoke this decision; instead, he had Marjorie confined in the Gilbertine nunnery at Watton in East Yorkshire.

What I have set down here represents the sum total of information I have been able to find about what befell the Bruce women. However, I thought about the locations where they were held. Roxburgh and Berwick Castles were both in Scotland, but very close to the border with England. Both were stocked with large English garrisons. It seemed obvious to me that Mary at Roxburgh and Isobel at Berwick were deliberately put there to taunt the Scots and perhaps to get King Robert, in his weakened situation, to make some vain rescue attempt.

I began to look at maps showing the places where the Queen, Princess Marjorie and Christian were held: all were all in the north of England, but not so deep enough in the country that when the Scots managed to re-organise they would not seem like tempting targets for a hit-and-run raid – especially so with the location of Queen Elizabeth's imprisonment: even a cursory glance at a map shows what a trap it would be to try and make an excursion into the Holderness peninsula, and how easily the Scots could be cut off and wiped out. King Edward had been especially cunning in his imprisonment of the Queen of Scots. She would be held captive for several years, her most productive for child-bearing. If she had been slain outright, Bruce could have remarried, but in those days there were no grounds for divorce. Her imprisonment therefore meant that she was far less likely to produce a heir if ever she and the King of Scots were reunited (and I'm sure Edward saw the chances of that happening as being very slim indeed!). He hoped to ensure that the Bruce dynasty would end with the death of Robert and so weaken any future struggle for an independent Scotland under its own monarchy.

Christian Bruce was confined in the Gilbertine nunnery at Sixhills, while Marjorie was eventually confined in the Gilbertine nunnery at Watton. I had heard of the various orders of religious establishments, like Cistercian or Carthusian, but Gilbertine was unknown to me.

Why Gilbertine establishments?

The order was established by Gilbert, a parish priest, in Sempringham, Lincolnshire, in the year 1130. He was later canonised and so is known in the annals as St Gilbert. The only wholly English religious order, it was unusual in that it included both males and females, segregated, of course. The order survived up till the Dissolution of the Monasteries in England under Henry VIII.

The only wholly English order. So that explained it! Other religious orders in England had their bases in other countries; for instance, the Clunaic monks, whose order originated at Cluny in France. Incarcerating these women in Gilbertine establishments meant that as an English order, under King Edward, there would be no complaining on their behalf as might have occurred if there were a foreign influence in a position of authority.

All that remained was to visit the sites of their incarceration. Although I already knew Roxburgh and Berwick intimately, I knew nothing of the others, so one summer's day in 2008 I decided to fire up my motorcycle and go on a little pilgrimage to visit the places where my countrywomen had been imprisoned so many years before, and at least look out over the surrounding landscape as they once did. I did not know what to expect, or whether I would find remains or even be able to locate the sites, but I knew I could stop and ask people who might have local knowledge. I was armed with nothing more than an ordinary road atlas.

It was to prove to be an enlightening and informative journey. I have always had a 'nose' for finding locations. A certain amount of luck is always involved, and I always seem to be lucky in the folk I encounter and ask for information. I came north from this particular trip with a wealth of new knowledge and some priceless photos in my camera.

It was cloudy, but the heavens did not open, so I was also lucky in that respect. I crossed the border in the west, then took the A69 east towards Newcastle, passing a myriad of places associated with the long history of war between Scotland and England. I took the M1 south. I was driving a 1200cc BMW bike, so I set it cruise control, let the big engine eat the miles and took in the landscape.

I passed Thirsk, where James Douglas eventually exacted a terrible retribution on the English at Myton and with his king at Byland. Bruce's ladies would have known of Douglas, at this point in his career a young knight; he had apparently shown a flair for finding food when they were on the run after Methven, and perhaps they saw the promise in this young man and knew that in him Scotland had a future champion. As I passed to the south of the Hambleton Hills I could see the huge, white horse carved in the chalky hillside over to my left.

At York I took the A166 so that I could stop and take in the site of the Battle of Stamford Bridge, fought in 1066, just a few weeks before the more famous Battle of Hastings. Then I continued east to the town of Driffield, where I took the A164 for Beverley and on to Watton. The A164 cuts through the tiny village, basically making it a village of two halves! But I turned into the eastern portion, where I spotted an old church that looked interesting.

I parked the bike at the entrance and went through the gate, crossing the little stream that followed the church boundary into the old graveyard. St Mary's looked very ancient at first glance, but closer inspection dated it to the 1500s. It was a very attractive little place and from the graveyard I got a glimpse of a jaw-dropping building over to my right. I jumped the wall and took in this amazing edifice. Some of the stonework was very old indeed, and I knew right away that this must have been part of the Gilbertine establishment where the Princess of Scotland had been kept. It is one of the most extraordinary houses I have ever seen.

The priory was founded in 1150 and it survived till 1539. I was later told that this remnant had been the prior's house, now a private dwelling known today as 'Watton Abbey'. I hadn't really expected to find any standing remains, so to see a building of this age and magnificence was a bonus.

Further scouting about revealed other bits and pieces, including old stonework with a running stream that looked like a medieval drain. There were other stone remains, but I don't think these were old enough to have been part of the original establishment. There was a nearby airfield during World War II and it was still possible to detect traces of this.

I was able to look over the landscape as Marjorie must have done in her captivity. She was still just a girl when she was brought here – not even a teenager. It must have been tough on one so young to have been isolated from her friends and family, living as a prisoner and enduring such an austere existence. I wonder how she perceived her father in all this? Was she bitter? Or did she understand that, as king, he had duties to his people and had to carry on the fight no matter what?

After taking some photos, I walked back to the bike, pleased to have made this connection to the early struggles of Robert the Bruce and had another location under my belt. As I turned the bike south again on the A164 I thought about King Robert and how he must have felt when the news of the fate of his womenfolk reached his ears. And not only of his womenfolk; the news of the hangings and beheadings of some of their escorts, including his brother, must have been the sort of hammer-blow from which few men would have been able to recover. This was part of the English plan to bring the Scots and their king to their knees. The painful sense of responsibility for so much suffering caused to loved ones would have proved overwhelming to most men. But Bruce was not just a man. He was a king. The King of Scots. And he would – he must – rise above this pain to continue the struggle for his country, not just for those in bondage, but for all those Scots who would be born in the years to come. He saw it as his duty to deliver their rightful legacy into their keeping.

Next I wished to see where Bruce's queen had been held. From Beverley I cut through the centre of Hull and turned east out to Hedon. The little village of Burstwick lay a few miles further on. I got there just before the school finished for the day, and there was a group of mothers waiting outside the gates for their children. It must have been a bit surreal when this large Scot pulled up on a bike and asked if any of them knew of an old manor house in the vicinity, or of any other old remains?

I basically caused much debate but got no answer to anything describing an old building in the vicinity of Burstwick. However, I was directed to some fish ponds near the village, as one lady thought they might be quite old. So I got back on the bike and wound my way to the ponds she had mentioned. There I met a fisherman who was not in the first flush of youth, so to speak, asked him if he was a local, told him I was searching for the remains of an old manor or castle, and did he

Left: The 'Maiden Stone', near Inverurie, Aberdeenshire.

Below: Memorial to Margaret Crawfurd of Crosbie, the mother of William Wallace.

HERE STOOD THE HOUSE OF
WILLIAM WALLACE
WHO IN LANARK IN 1297
FIRST DREW SWORD
TO FREE HIS NATIVE LAND

The great West Window in Dunfermline Abbey features Sir William Wallace, Malcolm Canmore; his wife, St Margaret of Scotland and King Robert the Bruce.

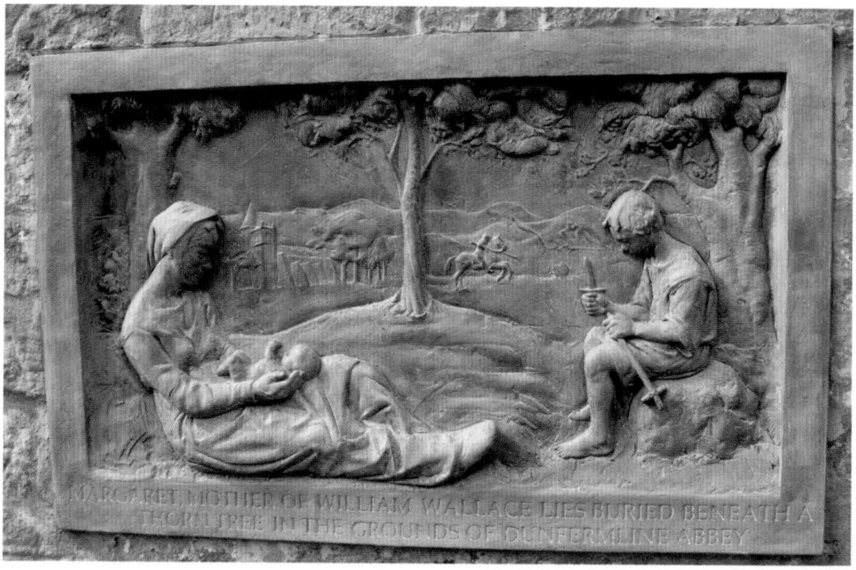

A beautiful plaque by artist Tim Chalk in memory of Margaret Crawfurd of Crosbie on a wall of the garden of the Abbot House, Dunfermline, bears the legend: 'Margaret, mother of William Wallace, lies buried beneath a thorn tree in the grounds of Dunfermline Abbey.'

The entrance to the cave where Margaret, wife of Malcolm Canmore, went for private prayer. King Malcolm is said to have built Dunfermline Abbey under her guidance.

A figure representing St Margaret praying in her cave retreat.

'Watton Abbey', now a private residence; this medieval building in East Yorkshire was formerly the prior's lodging at the nunnery where Edward I imprisoned Marjorie Bruce.

The tomb of Marjorie Bruce in Paisley Abbey. She died after a fall from her horse in 1316. The tomb was restored and erected in St Mirin's Aisle in 1817.

The ruins of Dunbar Castle where 'Black' Agnes, 4th Countess of Moray, stoutly, and with tremendous style, refused to surrender when placed under siege by the English in 1338.

The monument marking the site of the Carthusian Monastery in Perth. Here Joan Beaufort, wife of King James I of Scotland, was buried in 1445.

The graves in Dunblane Cathedral of the three sisters Margaret, Eupheme and Sibylla Drummond, who died in 1501 shortly after dining together, raising suspicions that they had been poisoned, perhaps because of Margaret's intimate relationship with King James IV.

In old Wigtown Graveyard Margaret McLachlan and Margaret Wilson lie alongside William Johnston, John Milroy and George Walker, three Covenanters hanged by Major Windram.

The memorial stone representing the stakes to which Wigtown martyrs Margaret McLachlan and Margaret Wilson were lashed on 11 May 1685, to drown in the incoming tide.

Plaque designed by Paisley sculptor Sandy Stoddart, recalling the hanging and burning of six women as witches in 1696.

A plaque at Balhaldie near the place where in 1746 a maidservant poured scalding water on the Duke of Cumberland, 'the Butcher'.

'Fair maiden Lilliard' who fought with ferocity against English raiders in 1545, was buried on the field of battle, on a ridge now known as 'Lilliards Edge', near Jedburgh.

St Kentigern's in Lanark, where Wallace is reputed to have married Marion Braidfute.

The Bridge of Doon where, as Robert Burns recounts, Tam o' Shanter made his escape from the clutches of a witches' coven he chanced upon in Alloway churchyard.

have any information? He thought for a minute, then said that he could recall that when he was a lad his father used to point to a farm and tell him that there was once a building near there where royalty used to stay. He had not thought about this for nigh on 60 years, but my asking had brought the memory back!

I asked where this farm was situated and was given directions. I jumped on the bike and headed a little out of the village to South Park Farm. I pulled into the farmyard, where I was greeted by a gentleman I took to be in residence. I asked him if this might once have been the site of an old castle or manor house.

'Yes,' he replied, 'an old manor stood here once.' And we spoke about the history of the place for a while.

The conversation ended with a bit of a bombshell from him.

'There are still some of the earthworks in the field right behind you. You can take photos if you want,' he added, glancing at my camera.

I walked the few yards over to the edge of the field. Slight contouring in the ground had hidden on the drive up what I could now see were very obvious traces: a mound and defensive works round about that might once have been a moat. Certainly there was still quite a bit of water in these man-made dips.

I took some photos and then just stood and looked around. Here I was, seven centuries on, standing where Queen Elizabeth, wife of the hero-king of Scots, had been incarcerated. I had never found anything written about her extended stay in England, beyond the fact that she was held at the manor of Burstwick. And this was the very spot.

There is something most gratifying to my Scottish soul, to see for myself the remnants of our history. Finding the site of the manor at South Park Farm was a spur to search further. The bits and pieces of information I later dug up might not be completely accurate, but they are interesting nonetheless. According to Thomas the Rymer's *Fœdera*:

> The Countess of Carrick, Queen of Robert Bruce, after the defeat of her noble husband in 1306, was consigned by Edward I to the care of Richard Oysel, steward of the royal manor of Holderness, at Burstwick. The king gave very explicit instructions as to her

treatment. She was to have with her two women of her own country, one a lady of honour and the other a chamber-maid, who were to be of good age and not gay; two pages who were also to be of good age and prudent, one of whom shall carve for her; a foot-boy to wait in her chamber, being sober, not a riotous person, to make her bed and perform such other offices as pertain to her chamber; a valet who shall be of good bearing and discreet, to keep the keys and serve in the pantry and cellar; and a cook. Three greyhounds were to be kept for her diversion in the warren and parks, and she was to have as much venison and fish as she should require.

George Poulson notes in *The History and Antiquity of the Seignory of Holderness* (1840) that:

Its site is said to have been visible on an eminence in the south park, with a moat surrounding it, in 1782... it is doubtful whether the moat may not be that which surrounded the old house that stood within it, and which forms nearly a square, comprising about four acres of land; the moat, although in some measure filled up, is easily defined.

Apparently, the south park retained its deer till 1722.

After absorbing as much as I could of my surroundings, and happy that I had been so fortunate in my quest, it was time to get back on the bike and head deeper into England, to continue with my pilgrimage and see what I could discover at the site of the imprisonment of Christian Bruce, widow of Sir Christopher Seaton, in Lincolnshire.

I took the A1033 back into Hull, and on towards the Humber Bridge. I could see it spanning the estuary ahead. I had never had cause to cross this major bridge before. Half watching the road and half turning my head to look up and down the river, I crossed into Lincolnshire and cut down to the town of Market Rasen, the name being familiar to me because of its famous racecourse. I then cut down a minor road to Sixhills.

Sixhills is a sleepy little place, a cluster of houses in hedged gardens sitting on a slight rise that gave views over the flat countryside. I rode the bike up and down its few leafy streets, looking for something to give me a clue as to the site of the establishment where Christian had been held. Sometimes a house- or street-name can give a clue, but I drew a blank. There were some old properties, but none dating back seven or eight centuries.

Eventually I stopped to speak to a man I had passed several times. He paused from cutting his hedge and said, 'I knew you were looking for something and wondered how long it would take you to pull up and ask. What is it you are looking for?'

I guess most folk don't really care about what happened in their area long ago and might think the questions I was about to ask were those of a madman. I hesitantly started to tell him I was interested in history and that there was once an old Gilbertine establishment in Sixhills and... but he broke in to tell me he knew a fair bit about local history, and that a large house I had passed on my way up the hill into the village was built on the site of the old Gilbertine religious centre. After a chat in which he told me some more about the history of Sixhills, I bade him farewell and turned back towards the house he had mentioned.

As you approach Sixhills from the north from the village of North Willingham, along Sixhills Road, just before the climb up to the village there is a large house over on the right called 'The Grange'. This residence sits on the site of the Gilbertine house. –

I was able to look over the landscape and 'see' the vista seen by Christian Bruce. Surrounded by the flat expanse of English countryside, far removed from the rolling hills of home, Christian must have wondered if she would be here for the rest of her days, not knowing or being informed of the situation in Scotland.

Before we move on, I'll touch on a wee twist in the history of this place. A monk called Robert Mannyng completed his chronicle in Sixhills in 1338. He had entered the order in 1288, having previously resided at other Gilbertine establishments in Lincolnshire. He mentions in his chronicle that he knew King Robert's brother Alexander well, having attended Cambridge with him in more peaceful times in the relationship between Scotland and England. It seems he had even met the future King of Scots when he hosted a party for his brother, which Mannyng attended. The English captured Alexander in southwest Scotland not long after Christian's arrival here and on the orders of King Edward he was hideously executed at Carlisle. And so Christian probably met a monk here who knew at least one of her brothers well.

That leaves the two women who were confined in cages hung over castle walls – Mary Bruce at Roxburgh, and Isobel, Countess of Buchan at Berwick – neither knowing how long they would be kept there, neither with any idea of the national situation, isolated, with no privacy from prying eyes and suffering the shouted abuse of their tormentors.

Roxburgh Castle stands on a large mound situated just before the confluence of the Rivers Tweed and Teviot, just above the town of Kelso. There are only scant ruins of stonework on the hilltop today, but a walk round the large site will give an idea of the scale of the original fortification, which was once surrounded by a water-filled ditch.

Berwick railway station stands in the middle of the remains of Berwick Castle. A walk out onto the platforms brings into view quite extensive stonework on the other side of the tracks. In Victorian times 'improvements' did not really take into consideration what already stood on the site and much of the remains of the castle's great hall was swept away for these new tracks.

The change in fortune for these women came unexpectedly, with Scotland's annihilation of Edward II of England's army on the field of Bannockburn in June 1314. Such a victory has repercussions, long after the clash of steel and the cries of wounded and dying men have faded. Bruce had captured so many high-ranking nobles that he was able to ransom them for the return of followers held captive in English prisons. The ransom of the Earl of Hereford was enough to return Bruce his womenfolk.

Elizabeth was to bear King Robert three children: Matilda, Margaret and David (who was to reign as King David II). She died on 27 October at Cullen in Banffshire while returning from a pilgrimage to St Duthac's in Tain, where she had been taken prisoner so many years before. She had gone back to give thanks for the turn in fortune in her life. We are told that she never really recovered from giving birth to her last child and a fall from her horse near Cullen caused internal bleeding that could not be stemmed. She was embalmed in Cullen and her entrails removed to be buried in the Lady Chapel of the church there. The old kirk near Cullen House stands on the site of this building and some of the stonework may well be remnants of the one that was here in Elizabeth's time. Although there is no memorial to her it is an interesting old place and well worth seeing. It does not have visiting hours as such and I was lucky that some of the staff were present when I went there. After I made a polite enquiry, they allowed me inside to have a look and take some photos.

Elizabeth's body was taken south to Dunfermline Abbey and she was buried near the high altar. When Robert died in 1329, he too was buried here. Elizabeth's body was seemingly rediscovered in February 1818. One of the earls of Elgin, who died in 1771, had had a monument erected to his memory. Where rebuilding work began, around 1818, it was decided to move this tomb to another part of the churchyard. This took place under the guidance of the then earl. During the course of this operation a stone vault was discovered that contained the skeleton of a lady, her long hair still preserved. It was supposed that this was Elizabeth.

The Earl of Elgin had this body removed I know not where – she may have been taken to a family vault or similar.

When she returned to Scotland, Princess Marjorie was in her late teens. She soon married King Robert's dashing young High Steward, Walter, who had distinguished himself on the field of battle at Bannockburn. She took up residence at his family home in the castle of Renfrew. This castle is long gone, the little mound where it stood is now a somewhat neglected children's park between the town's Ferry Road and Orchard Street, in Castlehill Crescent.

Shortly after their marriage Marjorie became pregnant. Pregnancy notwithstanding, she would often go out riding, which she must have particularly enjoyed after the long years spent in the confines of the nunnery at Watton. But one day in 1316, heavily pregnant, while riding between Renfrew and Paisley, she was thrown from her horse at Knock Hill, and died; her baby was saved. This child, the grandson of

King Robert, became the first of the Stewart dynasty of Scotland, King Robert II. The name of the Stewart dynasty comes from a corruption of the title of Marjorie's husband, Walter.

Marjorie's body was taken to Paisley Abbey to be buried. Her tomb stood for several centuries, until the then English Duchess of Beaufort, who wanted the building converted so that she could hear Anglican services, had it removed. Forlorn remnants lay in the abbey gardens, until in 1830 a minister of the church, Dr Boog, saw them and had it rebuilt, amalgamating pieces of similar tombs. This 'version' of Marjorie's tomb can still be visited within the abbey and there is also an ornate wall plaque in her memory.

An octagonal cross on a plinth of a few steps erected to mark the spot where Marjorie fell from her horse stood till 1779, when a local farmer, in his ignorance, used the pillar of the cross to form a door lintel and the stones of the plinth to repair a fence. But the site had not been forgotten: the father of Ian Hamilton, one of the party who 'liberated' the Stone of Destiny from Westminster Abbey in London in 1950, erected a large cairn to mark the spot. This cairn is on the right of Renfrew Road in Paisley as you drive towards Renfrew, on the edge of a housing estate called Gallowhill, a few hundred yards short of where the road crosses the M8.

Little is known of the later life of the other three captured women. Mary Bruce went on to marry a man by the name of Alexander Fraser in 1316. In 1326 Christian, the widow of Sir Christopher Seaton, married another great Scottish patriot, Andrew Murray, son of Wallace's companion of the same name. He died in 1338, but she went on to live well into old age, dying in 1357. We know even less of what became of Isobel, Countess of Buchan. But the fact that she knew where her patriotic duty for Scotland lay, and that she gave up all her security to crown the hero-king, has assured her an immortality with the hearts and minds of the people of Scotland.

CHAPTER 13
Black Agnes

I HEARD THE STORY of Black Agnes' defence of Dunbar Castle when I was a teenager. I admired her greatly then and it is a story I have loved to relate to others ever since. One of my earliest motorcycle forays was to Dunbar, to see the remains of the castle Agnes had so stoutly defended. I recall looking at the sea crashing against the rock stacks, climbing up into the heart of the ruins and gazing out over the landscape.

Agnes was born around 1312. Her father was one of Robert the Bruce's ablest lieutenants, Thomas Randolph, Earl of Moray (pronounced Murray). Thomas had led one of the divisions at Bannockburn in 1314, when Agnes would have just been a toddler. Along with James the Good – the famous Black Douglas – Thomas raided deep into England to try and get that country to recognise Scottish independence. Agnes, who must have been raised hearing the epic stories of these raids, grew up with such stalwart figures as Robert the Bruce and the Black Douglas playing significant roles in her life.

After Bruce's death in 1329 her father became the Regent of Scotland, but he only outlived his monarch by a few years, dying in Musselburgh on 20 July 1332. The house where he breathed his last, at the east end of the south side of the High Street, stood till 1809. As he lay on his deathbed, the people of the town gathered round, acting almost as a defensive shield; it is because of this that Musselburgh gained the appellation 'the Honest Town'. I wonder if Agnes, by then in her late teens, was present? Although it is likely that Thomas died from gallstones, the story circulated that the English had managed to administer poison to him. Certainly, although the English had signed the Treaty of Edinburgh in 1328 recognising Scotland's independence, they started to invade and exert their will before the ink on the document was dry. After her father's death Agnes became the 4th Countess of Moray. She gained the moniker 'Black' Agnes because of her mane of jet-black hair. She is said to have had an olive complexion.

Agnes married the Earl of Dunbar and March, and so was the

Lady of two Scottish earldoms. The English were constant aggressors, insistently trying to place Edward Balliol, son of the disgraced John Balliol (king of Scots from 1292 to 1296) on the throne of Scotland, using military might to oust David II, son of Robert the Bruce, from the throne.

While her husband was off fighting against the English, Agnes was left in charge of the castle at Dunbar. On 13 January 1338 a large English force under the command of Montague, Earl of Salisbury, appeared over the horizon and started to deploy for a major siege. A delegation came forward and ordered her to surrender the fortress, or suffer the consequences. Her bold retort is remembered in verse, as set down by the chronicler, Andrew Wynton:

> Of Scotland's King I haud my house,
> He pays me meat and fee,
> And I will keep my gude auld house,
> While my house will keep me.

The siege began in earnest, and the English brought forward engines called 'mangonels' and catapults capable of firing rocks and boulders against the castle walls with great force. Agnes gathered her ladies and told them to dress in their very best and meet her on the battlements. As the boulders rained down they stood nonchalantly, showing no fear, and when there was a near miss the one closest would draw out her handkerchief and flick away the dust. The English grew enraged at this insult, but they could not break their calm demeanour.

Several days went by and still the English attacks were failing to make the castle capitulate. Taking a different tack, Salisbury had a large battering ram, known commonly as a 'sow', brought up to smash in the castle doors. As the English began their work, Agnes cried, 'Beware Montague, for your sow may farrow!'

She then had her people drop a huge boulder from the castle walls. It smashed through the covering defence constructed above the ram. The surviving Englishmen beneath scattered, scrambling out and running for cover, Scottish arrows hastening their departure.

The English then adopted a dastardly course of action. They had captured Agnes' brother John, the Earl of Moray, and had him brought before the castle. Montague had it proclaimed that unless Agnes immediately surrendered the castle, John would be hung right there and then, before her eyes. He had assumed that her soft woman's heart would not allow such a thing, but he had met his match. Agnes simply laughed and said that the English could go ahead, for then she would inherit the Earldom of Moray and use its resources of manpower to fight the English invaders. Montague's bluff was called. John was spared. He went on to fight tirelessly for Scotland and was eventually slain on the field of Neville's Cross in 1346.

All other methods having failed, Montague decided that they should starve out the garrison. With the English forces arrayed before the castle there was no chance of relief coming from the Scottish forces. But the English had not reckoned on the pluck of Agnes. They sat it out for three months, waiting for the white flag of surrender, when one day Agnes sent out a messenger bearing a fresh baked loaf and some fine wine. Alexander Ramsay of Dalhousie had managed to bring two small boats laden with supplies from the Bass Rock to the castle's sea gate under cover of darkness; the garrison had been reprovisioned. The English realised that their quest was hopeless and started to pack up camp. This must have been galling for Montague, experienced soldier as he was.

Wynton finishes his rhyming tale of Agnes' defence with the lines:

She makes a stir in tower and trench,
that brawling, boisterous Scottish wench;
came I early, came I late,
I found Agnes at the gate.

Agnes and her husband did not have any children, so on her death in 1369 her inheritance passed to her nephews. Legend states that she was buried at Mordington, an estate a few miles to the west of Berwick upon Tweed granted by Robert the Bruce to her father, Thomas Randolph. Mordington House was a large establishment that had been added to over the centuries, the original pele tower becoming, in time, a large mansion. Unfortunately the place was demolished in 1973. An old burial vault survives nearby and it is here that Agnes is said to rest for eternity.

She is remembered in Dunbar though, with one of the town's hostelries on the approach to the harbour bearing the proud name 'Black Agnes' and her story is told on boards on the wall. The castle she defended so stoutly stood on several sea stacks, each connected by covered walkways. On my first visit I saw one of these walkways, like an old stone bridge arching from one stack to another; only a year or two later it had collapsed into the sea. Some of the castle ruins can be seen towering above the deep, narrow entrance channel to the harbour.

I have long been a huge fan of Agnes. A lady who knew where her loyalties lay and would not allow herself to be diverted from her duty where her nation was concerned. The spirit of her father was certainly running in her veins!

CHAPTER 14
Queen Joan Beaufort

THE FUTURE WIFE of James I of Scotland was born in 1404. She was the daughter of the Earl of Somerset and granddaughter of the famous Englishman, John of Gaunt, Earl of Lancaster, third son of Edward III. She was English by birth, but her story is reasonably well known in Scotland, more so than many of the queen consorts. It seems hers was a marriage of true love and not an arranged pairing, as was then so common among the nobility.

James I, who had been captured while en route to France in 1404, aged only 10, had been nominal king since 1406 when his father, Robert III, had died. As a royal captive in England, he was allowed access to various forms of education and he excelled in sport, poetry and music. He read all he could.

One day, looking from his tower window, he spotted a young woman strolling on the lawn outside. It seems she often walked this way, for every day James would linger at the window, hoping to catch a glimpse of her. He did not know her identity (her name was Joan Beaufort). He composed a poem dedicated to her, entitled 'The King's Quair', a lengthy work, very much in the style of Chaucer.

I have taken the liberty of modernising the words; one verse runs:

> And therewith I cast down my eye again,
> Where as I saw, walking under the tower,
> Full secretly new come here to play,
> The fairest or the freshest young flower,
> That ever I saw, I thought, before that hour,
> For which sudden abate, now astart,
> The blood of all my body to my heart.

James, though a captive, was a king, and it was agreed that Joan would be allowed to become his wife. They were married at Southwark Cathedral in 1424. Southwark is first mentioned in the Domesday Book of 1086, but the current structure was built between 1220 and 1420, so it is as it would have been at the time of the marriage.

The cathedral stands just at the south end of London Bridge, hence the name, a corruption of 'south work', as the bulk of the City of London stood on the north bank of the river. The modern London Bridge is just a few yards upstream from the ancient one. Thus, a King of Scots was married just a few yards away from where the head of the great patriot hero of Scotland, Sir William Wallace, was displayed on a spike after his gory murder at Smithfield.

On James and Joan's return to Scotland after a ransom payment of £40,000 for the king's person, a huge sum for those days, he was officially crowned at Scone. Joan would also have gone through some sort of crowning ceremony. James quickly set about restructuring Scotland's financial, legal and fiscal policy. He was a tireless worker and seems to have been advised constantly by Joan. During all this constructive work, Joan managed to bear eight children. Quite extraordinarily for those times, they nearly all survived into adulthood. Margaret, the eldest, married the Dauphin of France; Isabella married the Duke of Brittany; Eleanor married the Archduke of Austria; Mary became Countess of Buchan; Joan became Countess of Morton; Annabella became Countess of Huntly; and the first-born boy, James, became King James II of Scotland at only six years of age after his father's untimely murder. At birth, his twin brother Alexander had become Duke of Rothesay, the title automatically given to the heir to the throne, but he did not survive the first year of his life. In 1437 the queen was staying at the Blackfriars Monastery in Perth with her husband and ladies in waiting. It was a reasonably comfortable residence, and had a tennis court and James, being an athletic man, would often partake of the sport.

A visit to the ancient tennis court at Falkland Palace in Fife will show what the court at Perth must have looked like. The tennis balls were stuffed with feathers and were expensive to purchase; James lost them down a gap at one end of the court so often that he instructed some workmen to fill it up.

One night men clad in armour were heard approaching and there ensued the famous incident where Catherine used her arms to bar the door (fully described in the next chapter). Her selfless act gave the king the time to pull up some floorboards and drop into the sewer tunnel below. The boards were quickly put back in place and a rug was pulled over the top. As the assassins broke Catherine's arms and gained access, it is said that Queen Joan was wounded. Hindsight would probably have had the man wishing he had slain her out of hand. The apartments were searched and the route of the king's escape was soon discovered.

James had made his way along the tunnel only to find, to his horror, that the exit was blocked – this was the very gap his workmen had blocked up just a few days earlier. His assailants dropped into the tunnel and a desperate struggle ensued. James was unarmed, but he was muscular and strong and he fought his tormentors with his bare hands. But after receiving several stab wounds he collapsed and was repeatedly stabbed where he lay on the sewer floor.

Joan now came into her own. She had his killers hunted down and brought to justice. Sir Robert Graham led the murderers, but the Earl of Atholl and his grandson Robert Stewart, the Master of Atholl, had conceived the plot. Both men were relations of James; his grandfather Robert II had been married twice and as descendents of this second marriage they thought they had a right to the throne.

Joan was not to be appeased by a simple trial and execution to avenge the life of her beloved. For several weeks the guilty men were put through a living hell. One of a series of ingenious tortures involved these killers of a king being strapped to wooden thrones, whereupon iron crowns heated red hot in a furnace were then placed on their heads. Joan did have in her veins Plantagenet blood, from that line of English kings renowned in Scotland for their bestial cruelty. The murderers were eventually finished off by being beheaded by the axe – probably sweet release after their torments.

Joan eventually took a second husband. Two years later she married another James Stewart, the Black Knight of Lorne, and bore him three children. She died on 15 July 1445 and was buried in the Carthusian Monastery in Perth, beside King James. It was perhaps thought inappropriate that they should be buried in the Blackfriars Monastery after the events that had occurred there. But James had also been the founder of the Carthusian Monastery in Perth and may have had a particular fondness for the place.

The Carthusian Monastery is long gone. Like the Blackfriars Monastery it was destroyed at the time of the Reformation: both were looted and ruined in 1559 by a mob from Perth fired up by Protestant preachers. A monument marks the site of the place we can visit to forge a connection with Queen Joan. In the shape of a pillar, it stands at the junction of South Street and King Street and bears the inscription:

Within these grounds stood the Carthusian Monastery founded by King James I of Scotland in 1429. It was the only house belonging to this order in Scotland. In the precincts of the monastery were buried The Royal Founder, his Queen Joan Beaufort, and Margaret Tudor, Queen of James IV.

Just behind the monument is an interesting building which was originally constructed as a hospital but was converted into dwellings in the 19th century. Above the entrance is the inscription: 'Founded by King James VI in 1587'. This building, which sits on the site of the original monastery buildings, was largely reconstructed in 1750.

CHAPTER 15
Catherine Douglas

WHEN I WAS ABOUT 10 years old, I can recall a teacher at school telling us the story of Catherine Douglas. She did not call her Catherine, incidentally, but by the name she was commonly known throughout Scotland: Kate Bar-lass. This little talk was not part of the history curriculum, she just told us it as an aside, but it has been in my head ever since.

My classmates and I never got much in the way of Scottish history. We were taught about things like the Battle of Hastings – 1066 and all that. And, of course, the Battle of Hastings in this account was something that affected only England – and not Scotland. We were imbued with 'British' history, British meaning England. So when we learned something about the past of the Scots, it was like a light in the gloom. I can still remember all the Scottish-related snippets we were told.

I suppose we children were somewhat horrified at what Kate went through and probably winced as the story unfolded, but it was a story of bravery, and bravery carried out by a Scottish female was something we were not familiar with hearing.

And the story went like this...

Catherine Douglas was a lady in waiting for Joan Beaufort, queen consort of James I of Scotland. When King James was in Perth he liked to stay at the Blackfriars Monastery. It was probably far more comfortable than some draughty castle, and after all, he was with his wife, whom he adored. On 21 February 1437, James, his queen and her ladies, were relaxing and chatting in their quarters within the monastery, when the chink of armour was heard outside on the stairs. The king had enemies and the fact that men had somehow bypassed his guards to approach this room boded ill.

Queen Joan shouted to Catherine to bar the door. Catherine sprang forward to do so, only to find that the heavy wooden bar was missing. In those pre-lock days, doors were usually secured by putting a rectangular wooden bar into, or through, two iron staples at either side of the woodwork. Catherine, most likely panicking, and knowing that the suspected assailants were just feet away, thrust her arms through the staples to give James a few extra seconds to find a way to escape the confines of the room.

As described in the last chapter, he pulled up the floorboards, dropped into a drain and tried to make a getaway. Meanwhile, the assassins smashed at the door, probably confused as to how there was such a difficulty in opening it, knowing that the bar had been removed. Catherine gritted her teeth and suffered agony until one or both of her arms broke and the king's would-be murderers spilled in, ignoring the limp body of the girl on the floor.

Dante Gabriel Rosetti's poem 'The King's Tragedy', a lengthy work written in 1881, has some verses connected with this incident.

> Then the queen cried 'Catherine, keep the door, and I to this
> will suffice!'
> At her word I rose all dazed to my feet, and my heart was
> fire and ice.
> Like iron felt my arm, as through the staple I made it pass
> – alack! It was flesh and bone no more.
> 'Twas Catherine Douglas sprang to the door, but I fell back
> Kate Barlass.

Catherine survived her ordeal and her arms eventually healed. Whether she was disfigured by the incident we do not know, but she did go on to marry and have children. There are families of the surname Barlas in Scotland, who claim descent from Catherine Douglas. In the United States the expression 'Katy bar the door', meaning there is trouble ahead, take precautions, is said to stem from the tale of her brave deed.

Overlooking Perth's North Inch (a large area of parkland), at the junction of Charlotte Street and Blackfriars Street (an obvious clue!) there is a plaque on the wall about eight feet from the ground announcing that this was where Blackfriars Monastery was situated. In my book

Desire Lines I mention that this plaque was much defaced, with only a few words legible, and made the plea that if someone in authority happened to be reading, could they please see if the plaque could be renewed or replaced. A few months after the release of *Desire Lines* I again passed the site and was much gladdened to see that a plaque that looked shiny and new had been placed within the old stone surround of the original: people could once again read of the history that had happened on this spot. I don't know if my plea was responsible for the renewal, but if it was, I am flattered that I have done something for the good for Scotland!

The plaque does not mention the deed of Catherine, but tells how the monastery was founded in the days of Alexander II, how the 'battle of the North Inch' – a staged clan battle to settle a dispute – was fought opposite the monastery, watched by Robert II, and it tells of the stabbing to death of James I.

No matter. This is the place where Catherine Douglas barred the door and fell back with broken arms as Kate Bar-lass.

CHAPTER 16
Margaret Drummond

MARGARET DRUMMOND, A descendant of the second queen of David II, also named Margaret Drummond, was the eldest daughter of John, 1st Lord Drummond. Her family home was Drummond Castle near Crieff in Perthshire. She was probably born around 1475. Her beauty was such that, when she reached the age of 20 or so, she caught the eye of the then King of Scots, James IV.

Margaret certainly became James' mistress; there are records of her living at Stirling Castle in 1496, and, by James' personal invitation, at the Royal Palace of Linlithgow. In 1497 she bore him a daughter who was christened Margaret Stewart, therefore taking on her father's surname, as James was a member of the Stewart dynasty.

Many Kings of Scots had mistresses, James IV having had several whose names we know.

Much in the way of legend has built up over the years regarding Margaret Drummond. One abiding story is that she was not just James' mistress, but that they were secretly married, and that she was therefore Queen of Scots, and their daughter heir to the throne.

Kings were expected to marry into other European dynasties, thereby forging alliances and bonds with other nations. It is said that James, not wishing to be berated by the nobility of Scotland, secretly married the girl he loved, and not the one that he knew would be chosen on his behalf.

One unfortunate day in 1501 Margaret sat down to dinner in Drummond Castle with her two sisters, Eupheme and Sibylla. It was to be their last meal: all three succumbed to food poisoning, dying horrible deaths.

Although it seems there was not too much furore at the time, it has been claimed that certain Scottish nobles, wishing closer union with England, deliberately administered poison to the sisters, thereby allowing James to be available for the desired marriage to Margaret Tudor, daughter of the famous, or perhaps infamous, King Henry VII of England. This marriage did indeed take place, on 8 August 1503, in Holyrood Abbey in Edinburgh and was one of the main events that allowed James' great-grandson James VI to inherit the throne of England in 1603, thereby creating the Union of the Crowns that was to put the nation of Scotland in the position of the minor player in an unwelcome partnership.

A lot of evidence has been put forward to support the idea of the deliberate murder of Margaret Drummond. James continued to make provision for their daughter though the Drummonds were a wealthy family, and he paid for masses to be said for the soul of Margaret. Margaret and her sisters were buried before the high altar of Dunblane Cathedral, a place of some prominence. They lie there still, under three steely blue slabs with brass plaques attached, in the choir of the cathedral. I have often visited Dunblane Cathedral, and have never failed to pause at these stones and make a little mental connection with these three girls who died centuries before, asking myself, 'Was Margaret Queen of Scots?'

Dunblane Cathedral is certainly a place that merits a visit. It was founded by St Blane about 600 AD, hence its name. The prefix, Dun, means a fortification or a mound of some sort, and the Blane part takes its name from the saint. The lower four storeys of the tower are of the ancient Celtic edifice, the rest of the stonework on show dates from the mid-1200s. There was an attempt to remove the gravestones of Margaret and her sisters in 1817, but an outcry resulted in them being put back in place. I can only salute these Scots who made sure that a little piece of history was left *in situ* for future generations to visit, enjoy and understand.

There are other attractions within the cathedral, a place where you can sense the history: there are ancient carved Celtic crosses, some beautiful woodwork, and a memorial to the local children who were tragically gunned down in the massacre of more recent years. While walking round the churchyard, pause to look down to the River Allan which flows in a gorge below the cathedral.

Drummond Castle, is still owned by Margaret's descendents. The ornate gardens, which are open to the public, featured in the movie

Rob Roy, starring Liam Neeson in the title role; (in the movie they were the gardens of the residence of the Duke of Montrose, played by John Hurt).

King James IV died on the field of battle at the fateful Flodden Field on 9 September 1513. The greatest of the Stewart dynasty and truly loved by his people, he was a 'Renaissance prince' who delighted in the arts, encouraging the writers, poets and storytellers of his country and bringing them to a previously unheard-of prominence. He built a navy for Scotland, including his flagship, the *Great Michael*, in its day the largest warship in Europe.

His daughter with Margaret was to marry twice: she bore three children to her first husband, John, Lord Gordon; her second husband was a namesake of her mother, Sir John Drummond, and she bore him two children.

I suppose the descendents of these children are well aware of the fact. They must wonder at the validity of the stories of the marriage of James IV and Margaret Drummond, for if the legends are true, then they are legitimate claimants of the royal line of Scotland.

CHAPTER 17

Lilliard

I CAN'T REMEMBER how and when I first heard the story of Lilliard. It is one of those stories that kids in Scotland get as part of their heritage. I knew it from quite a young age, but can't recollect my mother telling me it, or reading about it, but Lilliard's tale was sort of embedded in me at a young age, and it gave me respect for the patriotism that beats in the heart of Scottish women.

The women of Scotland have been voracious in their hunger for independence, and have often been the movers and shakers in reminding their men where their loyalty should lie. It does not matter that Lilliard's story may be the stuff of legend, she represents thousands of Scotswomen down the centuries, who would not kneel or serve under the heel of a foreign oppressor. Interestingly, the story does not vary, no matter what source you glean it from. When stuff is woven from legend there tend to be variations in differing accounts, but this tale seems to be set in stone.

In the 16th century there was constant warfare spilling across the border between Scotland and England. The Scots had been heavily beaten at the Battle of Solway Moss on 24 November 1542 and it seems that the English were of the opinion that they could do what they wished on Scottish territory. And it seems they were quite justified in this. This was the time known as the 'Rough Wooing'. Henry VIII, he of the 'six wives', was on the throne of the southern nation. He was determined that Mary Queen of Scots, only a child, should be wed to his son Edward. Henry knew that the greater, in most cases, absorbs the lesser, and he knew that such a marriage would more than likely eventually bring Scotland under England's sway.

The Scots resisted these attacks as best they could, determined, no matter how bad the English depredations, that they would not allow their nation to be coerced. Some of these depredations were terrible indeed. Sir Ralph Eure burnt Brumehouse Tower when the lady of the place would not surrender to his Englishmen and she and her children perished in the flames. The Earl of Hereford during one raid vandalised the tombs of the Douglas Earl of Angus and wasted his lands. He devastated Edinburgh and its port of Leith. As you can imagine, Scotsmen were itching for revenge.

The English again raided in strength in 1545. Moving north from the town of Jedburgh, they encamped at Ancrum Moor. Their army of 5,000 men, comprised mostly of English borderers, was bolstered by German and Spanish mercenaries and, shamefully, by several hundred Scottish borderers who had agreed to fight for King Henry after the debacle of Solway Moss. They were led by the aforementioned Eure and his co-commander Sir Brian Layton.

The Earl of Arran, James Hamilton, and Archie Douglas, Earl of Angus managed to raise some 1,500 men and hearing of the English whereabouts, decided to see what they could do to confront the enemy. Scott of Buccleuch, who was a daring soldier and led many border Scots who had much raiding experience, joined them. His input would be vital. It was suggested that a party of Scots would attack the English camp and see if they could lead them into a trap. This feint did indeed cause the bulk of the English army to head off in pursuit, but as they came over the top of the ridge now known as Lilliard's Edge, the Scottish forces were lying in wait.

The English were facing the setting sun, the smoke of the Scots guns blew into their faces and they became disorientated. In the front ranks of the Scottish lines stood a fair maiden, Lilliard by name, who, sword in hand, fought with extraordinary ferocity. We are told that her lover had been slain in an English raid, and she had sworn revenge. Lilliard cut down every Englishman that came near her and though she gained serious wounds as the battle went on, she would not relinquish her position. The Scots who had originally been in the English ranks suddenly remembered what blood flowed in their veins, and rejoined their countrymen. It was the last straw, and despite their large superiority in numbers, the English lines began to buckle and crack. They left 800 dead on the field.

Poor Lilliard succumbed to her wounds. It is claimed that the Scots scoured through the bodies to find this girl whose name was already being repeated with awe among the victors and that she was found beside the dead form of Layton – one of her final acts had been to cut down one of the English commanders.

She was buried on the high ridge of the field of battle, since known as Lilliard's Edge in honour of her unshakeable position on the height. A gravestone marked the spot. Though by the 1700s the inscription had become somewhat weatherworn, a local minister, the Reverend Adams Milne, was able to consult elderly locals who remembered it. It ran as follows:

> Fair Maiden Lilliard
> Lies under this stane.
> Little was her stature,
> But muckle was her fame.
> Upon the English loons,
> She laid monie thumps.
> And when her legs were cuttid off,
> She fought upon her stumps. AD 1545.

At the beginning of April 2009 there was a spell of beautiful weather. That was my cue to fire the bike up and go and get some of the photos I needed for this book. Tootling round a bend, I hit a pothole and got thrown off the bike and did a hell of a lot of damage to the front end. Any one you walk away from is a good one, right enough; I tried to hide my shame and anger at coming off and pushed on to Ancrum regardless, determined to fulfil my purpose and get pictures of Lilliard's grave.

The battle of Ancrum Moor was fought to the east of the A68, about two miles north of the village of Ancrum itself. As you pass the farm of Lilliard's Edge you are looking over the rise where the main action took place.

A Roman Road, Dere Street, dissects the field; this now forms part of 'St Cuthbert's Way'. An Ordnance Survey Landranger 74 map is a handy tool to see where it is possible to gain access to the footpath;

Lilliard's grave is marked simply as 'stone' on the edge of the field with the crossed swords symbol. The footpath can be pretty muddy, so appropriate footwear is recommended.

I climbed up to the summit of the ridge where a new information board tells the story of the battle. While it also recounts Lilliard's part in it, it may be seen as going some way to exploding her whole myth with the information that there was a cross on this site in 1372, known as Lylliard's Cross – implying that the name predates the battle.

There is also a stone here with a metal plaque which gives more information on Lilliard, but it is quite difficult to read. Her grave is just on the other side of the fence, where you cross a stile to gain access: it is a rectangular structure, with a stone giving the same verse as above, erected to replace the old one, now long gone.

There is a stone on the front of the grave, its inscription a little worn. Lady John Scott, who wrote a version of that famous song 'Annie Laurie', put this in place. She had been responsible for the refurbishment of the grave. This stone bears the inscription:

> TO A' TRUE SCOTSMEN.
> By me it's been mendit
> To your care I commend it.

I sat up here on the ridge and just took in the beauty of the view. To the north were the Eildon Hills, to the south, the Cheviots, the hills of England in the distance. It was such a clear day the visibility was superb. Just beside me, Dere Street ran away in either direction, its route clearly discernible across the landscape, marked by the trees that had been allowed to grow along its course. The battlefield sloped away to the north. It was easy to imagine men (and a woman!) locked in a vicious battle. Lilliard's Edge Farm sat at the bottom of the slope, and beyond it, mile after mile of rolling countryside steeped in history. Lying in the grass alongside Lilliard, it was hard to snap myself out of my reverie and begin the walk back down the slope. I hope if you visit you have an equally memorable day.

CHAPTER 18
The Wigtown Martyrs

THE STORY OF THE WOMEN known as the 'Wigtown martyrs' horrified me when I heard it as a boy, and that horror has not lessened over the years, partly because of what they must have experienced in their last moments, and partly because supposedly intelligent human beings could inflict such a death in the name of justice.

Wigtown is in southwest Scotland, in an area known as the 'Machars', a little peninsula that juts into the Solway Firth. There is a town in Cumbria in England called Wigton, and the name probably has the same source: 'the village on the hill'. Wigtown has often been called Wigton in the past, but it tends to be called Wigtown today, which avoids confusion.

The story I'm about to tell took place during 'the killing time', a phrase coined by Robert Wodrow in his *History of the Sufferings of the Church of Scotland* which has since become widely used, and appears in most of our history books.

The date is 1685; the ladies in question here are Margaret McLachlan, a woman of 63, and 18-year-old Margaret Wilson, both devout Covenanters. Scotland was a Presbyterian country, but the monarchy in England was Episcopalian, and the king there was determined that the Scots too would come under the umbrella of this form of worship. Scots, determined to oppose any controls over the right to worship in their own way, became involved in a struggle that was both theological and political.

Those who opposed English oppression became known as Covenanters, the name originally coming from a document, or covenant, signed to demand religious freedom. Covenanters, unable to worship in the Kirk and threatened with military intervention, began to gather in remote spots, often out on the moorland of southern Scotland, for meetings called 'conventicles'. They risked being killed if their participation was discovered. There are monuments to Covenanters scattered all over Scotland and the graves of many of these martyrs are still tended regularly. A book I can recommend as a guide to Covenanting sites is *Standing Witnesses* by Thorbjorn Campbell. My own well-used copy has gone with me on many of my travels through Scotland.

The crown demanded that Scots take an oath to the king, but the Presbyterians would take no oath or bend the knee to anyone but God himself. In particular, the Scots' pride rejected the humiliation of taking any kind of oath to a hierarchy centred in London, the capital of a foreign power. Because of their refusal to submit, the two Margarets were arrested, along with the younger Margaret's 13-year-old sister Agnes and another woman by the name of Margaret Maxwell. Margaret Maxwell took the oath to the king and was therefore set free. The two younger girls' father, Gilbert Wilson of Glenvernock, near Penningham, frantically put together a bond payment to try and secure their release. Many friends and sympathisers contributed and a hundred pounds was raised. Though it was a vast sum for those times, he was informed that it was only enough to obtain the release of Agnes.

At the trial of the two Margarets some wild accusations were made. It was claimed that they had been present at the Battle of Bothwell Bridge and at the encounter at Airdsmoss that had taken place several years before, when the younger Margaret would have been nothing more than a small child.

A recent law had been passed to allow the public drowning of Covenanter women and it was judged that this was to be the fate of the two unyielding Margarets. Men accused of the same crime were usually hung, but for some reason the powers-that-be felt there should be a different punishment for the different sexes. The two women were to be tied to wooden posts fixed in the sand of the tidal estuary of the River Bladnoch where it flows into the Solway Firth; the incoming tide would therefore overwhelm them and they would drown slowly, gasping for breath between the rising waves, till their mouths were covered and they could breathe no more.

It seems that the Privy Council of Scotland, perhaps embarrassed at the barbarity of this sentence, ordered a stay of execution on 30 April 1685, but one of the commission who found the two Margarets guilty was the notorious Sir Robert Grierson of Lagg, who was known for his hatred of the Covenanters. We can be sure that he would have done all in his power to see that 'justice' was carried out.

At low tide on 11 May 1685 the women were tied to posts erected on the sand, the older woman a little further out so that she would drown first. The accusers hoped that this would terrify the girl into taking the oath to the king in London. Wodrow describes the scene:

> The two women were brought from Wigton, with a numerous crowd of spectators to see so extraordinary an execution. Major Windram with some soldiers guarded them to the place of execution. The old woman's stake was a good way in beyond the other, and she was first despatched, in order to terrify the other to a compliance with such oaths and conditions, as they required. But in vain, for she adhered to her principles with an unshaken steadfastness. When the water was overflowing her fellow martyr some about Margaret Wilson asked her what she thought of the other now struggling with the pangs of death. She answered, 'What do I see but Christ [in one of his members] wrestling there. Think you that we are the sufferers? No, it is Christ in us, for he sends none a warfare upon their own charges.'
>
> When Margaret Wilson was at the stake, she sang the 25th psalm from verse 7th, downward a good way, and read the 8th chapter to the Romans with a great deal of cheerfulness, and then prayed.
>
> While she was at prayer, the water covered her; but before she was quite dead, they pulled her up and held her out of the water till she was recovered, and able to speak; and then by Major Windram's orders, she was asked, if she would pray for the king. She answered [in reference to the elder Margaret], 'She wished the salvation of all men, and the damnation of none.' One [soldier] deeply affected with the death of the other and her case, said, 'Dear Margaret, say God save the king, say God save the king!' She answered in the greatest steadiness and composure, 'God save him, for it is his salvation I desire'. Whereupon, some of her relatives nearby, desirous to have her life spared, if possible, called out to Major Windram, 'Sir, she hath

> said it, she hath said it!' Whereupon the major came near, and offered her abjuration, charging her instantly to swear it, otherwise return to the water. Most deliberately she refused, and said, 'I will not, I am one of Christ's children, let me go.' Upon which she was thrust down again into the water, where she finished her course with joy.

There is a weird little local legend connected with the last moments of these ladies' lives recounted in Robert Chambers' *The Picture of Scotland* (1827). The town officer is said to have pressed them down into the water with his halberd, a long-poled axe. He would ask them if they would swear the oath, and when they shook their heads in denial, he would cry, 'Then take another drink, me hearties!'

It is told that divine providence then came into the equation, and from the moment of their deaths he developed an unnatural thirst and could not stop drinking; he was afflicted with having to carry a large jug of water with him everywhere he went.

After their bodies were cut from the posts, the two Margarets were buried in the local churchyard, where they lie today. Major Windram hanged three male Covenanters around the same time. William Johnston, John Milroy and George Walker also lie in the churchyard, and their commemoration stone today lies beside that of the two Margarets. The grave of Margaret McLauchlan bears the following inscription:

> Memento Mori. Here lyes Margaret Lachlane who was by unjust law sentenced to die by Lagg, Strachane, Winrame and Grahame and tyed to a stake within the flood for her adherence to Scotland's reformation covenants national and solemn league aged 63. 1685.

Some sources say that in reality she was about 70 years of age, but the stone does claim 63. The younger Margaret's stone bears an inscription, which includes this passage:

> Let earth and stone still witness bear, their lyes a virgine martyre here. Murther'd for ouning Christ supreame, head of his church and no more crime. But not abjuring presbytery and her not ouning prelacy.

The three stones of those martyred lie together in the old churchyard of Wigtown within a railed enclosure. There is also a large obelisk on the outskirts of the town in their memory. Most poignant, though, is the stone representing one of the stakes that the women were tied to, which stands on the site of their actual suffering. The River Bladnoch has changed course a little over the centuries, and so this monument stands on dry land.

There is also a monument to the two Margarets in the graveyard of the Holy Rood church in Stirling. It stands in an area of the burial ground known as the 'valley', where in medieval times, the ladies of the court would watch the jousting contests that took place when the king was in residence at Stirling Castle. This monument is in the shape of a cupola with statues within.

Probably the oddest postscript to this story is the way that artists have depicted Margaret Wilson in the centuries since her death. In the Walker Art Gallery in Liverpool there is a painting of her, tied to her stake, the waters rising to her waist. She is depicted as buxom and pretty with a mane of thick blond hair, her hands tied behind her back. When the painting was X-rayed in recent years, it was discovered that the artist had originally painted her naked, but clothes had been added at a later date in deference to Victorian sensibilities.

There is also a marble statue of her in Knox College, Toronto, Canada. In this version her hands are tied before her; again she has a flowing mane of hair reaching her waist, but she is bare-breasted. Strange as it seems for a subject who died such an unsavoury death, her depiction is undoubtedly sexy. I think the deeply religious Margaret would be bemused to see how her story has been perceived over the centuries!

Most visitors to Wigtown will drive into the village from the north, on the A714. As you come up the last rise into Wigtown, you will see the large, tall obelisk off to your right atop a grassy mound. At first glance it looks as if it stands in the middle of a field, but if you take the first right on driving into the town and then take the first right again, you will find signposted a mossy, sunken lane that leads right up to the monument, which is on your left, with an inshot for parking on your right. There is a great view over the town and the Solway Firth from this elevated position.

On returning to the main road, turn right to continue into the centre of the town. You come to a T-junction at the village green. A left turn will take you downhill to the church. The older church is a picturesque ruin in the old graveyard, alongside its more modern counterpart. The graves of the Wigtown martyrs, both male and female, stand on the far side of the ruins in their own little enclosure.

Further down the hill a parking area is signposted. Once parked here among the trees and facing out to the firth, you will see a footpath branching off to your right. Just a few yards along, a gate takes you out onto the marshland. It is very boggy, but there is a wooden walkway leading to the stone monument, shaped symbolically like a stake, that marks the spot where according to local tradition the two Margarets suffered for their beliefs. Time has changed the route of the waterways in this area, and so the 'stake' stands inland from the sea today, but it is still a spot to stand and take in the vista of rolling hills and tidal flats, a haven for wading birds – and for us to go and think of the poor women who suffered here.

CHAPTER 19
Witches in Scotland

SCOTLAND IS A COUNTRY seen internationally as having a long association with witches. This is largely due to Shakespeare's *Macbeth* with its three witches, or 'weird sisters' as they are sometimes known; and also to the poem 'Tam o' Shanter' by Scotland's national bard, Robert Burns, with its story of Tam accidentally coming across a coven.

Belief in witchcraft lasted into fairly modern times in Scotland: in rural areas, especially in the Highlands, folk might claim that a neighbour had put the 'evil eye' on their cattle so that they did not produce milk, or attribute various illnesses to the influence of a local witch.

On my travels round the country, always by chance, I have come across places with a 'magical' association. All but a few of these places are where witches suffered for their craft. I think it's that old adage that if you do something good, no one remembers, but if something bad happens, no one forgets. And local communities seem to remember where witches suffered, more than for any other reason.

We should never forget the torture and suffering involved in accusations of witchcraft. The number of women who were drowned or burnt after sessions of sleep deprivation and insertions of needles and the like to elicit confessions from folk maddened with pain, is a stain on our history. Ducking Pools, where suspected witches were tied to chairs and suspended underwater, or thrown in to ascertain if they were witches or not, abound in Scotland. If they sank and drowned they were deemed innocent, if they floated they were deemed to be witches. So it was tails you lose, heads you lose. The stream near to my house in East Kilbride has the site of a 'Witches Pool' where such 'trials' were carried out. The number of women killed in such ways is well into four figures, although estimates vary. The charges brought were outrageous. One witch was accused of turning her daughter into a pony, having her shod, and riding her about town. Really, what is the point? If you had magical powers you might as well have used them to further your community, or in this day and age, to choose the winning lottery numbers. But turning family members into animals? Yet supposedly educated men debated the life or death of a woman on the truth of such matters.

So let's look at a few of the locations around the landscape of Scotland where there are associations with the supernatural.

Although the witches in *Macbeth* are in a work of fiction, albeit based on a 'true story' with the various liberties of the truth that 'based on a true story' invariably involves, the place where they gave their prophecy to Macbeth is pointed out. Near to the village of Brodie on the A96 Aberdeen to Inverness road, a sign points the way, a mile and a quarter north to 'Macbeth's Hillock'. Just a few miles east lies the town of Forres. If you park near the police station, you will see at the roadside in front of the building there is an inscription telling you that you are standing before the 'Witch's Stone'. A couple of hundred years ago someone started to break up this stone for building purposes, but there was an outcry and the pieces are held together today by iron staples. Directly behind the police station rise the steep flanks of Cluny Hill. Unfortunate women accused of witchcraft were taken to the hilltop, put into a barrel through which iron spikes had been driven, and then the top was nailed into place and the barrel set bouncing down this hill. The occupant was impaled and mangled by the spikes and when the barrel came to a halt, tar and pitch would be added and the whole mess burnt to ashes. The Witch's Stone marks the spot where one barrel came to rest and was then burnt.

King James VI had a peculiar interest in witches. Witch trials and slayings reached a peak during his reign. Strange that he is also the man who brought into being the 'King James Version' of the Bible – had it translated from the ancient scriptures into the more accessible version we have today. James saw Satanic plots in every situation. He had a slovenly shambling gait, but was a very learned individual too; this has led to his being nicknamed 'the Wisest Fool in Christendom'.

James had sailed to Denmark to bring home his new queen, Anne. While they were crossing back to Scotland across the North Sea a huge storm blew up, which he claimed was the work of witches. Witnesses were found who testified that 94 witches and six wizards had summoned up this storm in the kirk in North Berwick. One of the witches, Gelie Duncan, played the Jews Harp (a little metal mouth instrument that I believe may be called a jaw's harp elsewhere in the world) while the rest of the coven danced about the churchyard. At the trial in 1591 it was stated:

> The Devil started up himself in the pulpit, like ane meikle [big] black man, and called everyone by name, and every ane answerit 'Here Master'. On his command they openit up the graves, twa within, and ane without the kirk, and took off the joints of their fingers, taes, and knees and partit them amang them.

You can go to North Berwick to the ruins of the Auld Kirk and stand and imagine the Devil himself rising up in the pulpit. Its site was once on a sandy islet connected to the mainland by an arched bridge, but various extensions to the harbour area have assured that the site is today attached firmly to the mainland.

The bulk of the witches who suffered in Scotland did so on what is known today as Edinburgh Castle Esplanade. It is possible that as many as 300 women were hanged or strangled and their bodies burnt here. It now throngs with tourists and the world famous Edinburgh Military Tattoo is held on it, with thousands watching from the tiers of seating that are built specially for the spectacle each year. But once crowds gathered here to see the spectacle of witch-burning taking place before the main gates of Edinburgh Castle.

One of the most famous witches in Scotland's history is Isobel Gowdie. She lived in the village of Auldearn, close to Forres. I first heard her name when I was at school, as it was the title of a track on an album by the Sensational Alex Harvey Band, one of the biggest rock acts to emerge from Scotland in the 1970s. She has also appeared as a character in several novels, and James MacMillan has composed an orchestral piece entitled *The Confession of Isobel Gowdie.*

Isobel, who was tried in 1662, does not seem to have been tortured or suffered harm afterwards. She gave a very detailed account of life as a witch, describing how she could incant a spell to transform into a hare and how she could utilise an ordinary broom to make it fly. Perhaps the picture that comes to our mind of witches in capes with pointy hats and flying on broomsticks can be partially attributed to Isobel.

Paisley has a poignant reminder of the days of witches and covens. Christian Shaw was the 11-year-old daughter of the Laird of Bargarran. In 1696 she began to have fits and it is said she brought up lumps of hair, coal, straw and gravel. The girl accused a family servant, Catherine Campbell, of putting a spell on her. Eventually a total of six people were to suffer by the command of Lord Blantyre, the head of the commission appointed by the Privy Council of Scotland in what I believe to have been the last multiple trial for witchcraft held in Europe. These sham trials were headed by the top minds of the realm, which seems unbelievable to our modern sensibilities. Two of those condemned to die were brothers, John and James Lindsay, aged only 11 and 14 respectively; it is reported that they held hands as they were hung. The other four were women. Catherine Campbell was carried screaming to the town's Gallow Green where along with Margaret Fulton, Margaret Lang and Agnes Naismith, she was hung. Their bodies were then taken to Maxwellton Cross to be burned. A horseshoe was set into the spot where this burning took place and where their remains were afterwards buried, in the belief that such an act would forbid the spirits of those condemned from rising and troubling the living. Traditions sprang up that if the horseshoe were to ever disappear, the town would suffer a decline.

The horseshoe did eventually disappear, in the 1970s, and on 9 May 2008 a new monument to mark the spot was unveiled. It was created by local sculptor Sandy Stoddard, who freely gave of his time and talent to help his local community and to keep a little of the town's history intact. This memorial, in the centre of the busy junction of Maxwellton Street and George Street, comprises of a stainless-steel horseshoe set into a circular plate which bears the words: 'Pain Inflicted, Suffering Endured, Injustice Done'.

If you wish to have a quick look at this memorial, or wish to photograph it, I can only suggest you copy what I did! And that was to press the button to operate the pedestrian crossing, and you will have a few seconds to act while the traffic comes to a halt at the ensuing red traffic lights.

Dornoch was the site of the last witch-burning in Scotland – of Janet Home, the woman charged with changing her daughter into a pony. It seems her burning in a tar barrel took place in 1727. The stone that marks the site stands in a garden on your left as you drive out towards the towns' golf course (although it bears the date 1722).

The site I came across on my travels that sticks in my mind most strongly is the monument to Maggie Wall. Dunning is signposted from the A9 south of Perth. From the centre of Dunning take the Auchterarder road and about a mile out of the village on the right-hand side there is a little gap in the wall; several yards back there is a monument in the shape of a cairn, with a pillar protruding from the top and a cross atop the pillar. In white on the front of the stonework it proclaims: 'Maggie Wall, burnt here 1657 as a witch'. The paintwork is regularly freshened, though no one seems sure who is responsible and apparently no one has ever seen it being done.

History books do tell of several witch-burnings in this area, but none concern a Maggie Wall. Perhaps she was the victim of a lynch mob, who with retrospective regret erected this monument to her memory.

Robert Burns' epic poem, 'Tam o' Shanter' tells of Tam leaving a local bar to ride home on Meg, his grey mare, and happening across a coven. Tam watches as a buxom young witch, clad only in a revealing shirt, dances to bagpipes played by the Earl o' Hell himself. When she finishes, Tam can't help but shout 'Weel done Cutty Sark!' (A cutty sark was a type of short shirt made of fine linen.) The witches then chase Tam, who desperately gallops for a bridge over running water – it was popularly believed that witches, when practising their art, could not cross running water. Cutty Sark manages to grab Meg's tail, which comes away in her hand, but Tam is lucky enough to get away by inches. Although a work of fiction, the places in the poem do exist and can be visited today.

Tam was a real character too, and a friend of Burns. His grave is in the churchyard of Kirkoswald in Ayrshire, the graves clustered round the ruins of the ancient church named after St Oswald, and said to be the place where Robert the Bruce was baptised in the ancient stone font in the body of the church.

The church where Tam watched the witches is Alloway Kirk, now picturesque ruin in the village of Alloway south of Ayr; a few hundred yards past the church is the old Bridge of Doon where Tam made his escape from his pursuers. It is a pleasure to stand on this old bridge and imagine Tam galloping for all he is worth down the hill from the kirk, and, turning onto the bridge to head towards you, the witches in full flight at his back. A place to visit that I'm sure you will never forget!

CHAPTER 20
Jenny Geddes

THE STORY OF JENNY GEDDES is widely known in Scotland, but there are some who say that her story is nothing but a fable. However, it is so well known, and told time and again without variation, that there is a real ring of truth to it.

Jenny is accredited with a deed that caused a riot that set in motion a chain of events that led to the Wars of the Covenant, the Wars of the Three Kingdoms, the English Civil War, and the execution by beheading of King Charles I in London's Whitehall, and Oliver Cromwell's harsh occupation of Scotland.

Mayhem.

Wow! What a girl!

She was reputedly born in 1600 and lived till about 1660, plying her trade as a street fruitseller in Edinburgh's Royal Mile and environs. Such lowly members of church congregations as Jenny did not have seats in the pews. They either took their own little stools to sit on in front of the pulpit, or for a small fee, they would hold a place for their 'betters', so ensuring they got a good space with a view. Jenny was a regular attendee of St Giles Cathedral in Edinburgh.

The Reformation of the Church in Scotland came about in 1560, with the emphasis of religion in the country changing from Roman Catholicism to Presbyterianism. The Scots adopted a stern, hard Calvinism, with a more puritan attitude than the churches in England. King Charles I, though born in 1600 at the Palace of Dunfermline in Scotland, had been raised with English ideals, having lived in that country since 1604.

For his coronation ceremony at St Giles in 1633, he used an Anglican service. This did not endear him to the ordinary people of Scotland, who saw Anglicism as a form of 'Popery'.

Charles believed in the Divine Right of Kings. This stubborn attitude was behind the move to have a book of common prayer drawn up for

Scotland, to bring the way religion was conducted in the country more in line with England. This book was to be used for the first time at a service in St Giles on Sunday 23 July 1637. There was real excitement in the air at this news.

Dean Hannah began to read the Collects, part of this new procedure, when Jenny Geddes suddenly shouted, 'Dare you say the Mass in my lug [ear]?' and threw her stool at his head, sparking off a riot in the church. The town guard helped to eject the rioters, Jenny included, and the service eventually continued, but to the accompaniment of banging on the doors and the sound of breaking glass as windows were smashed.

Word of these events soon got around and there was unrest and trouble at other Edinburgh churches. The unrest soon spread across Scotland and the Lord Advocate of Scotland put together a committee who beseeched King Charles to withdraw the hugely unpopular Anglican service from Scotland. Charles refused. The Scots, determined to keep their right to worship in their own chosen style drew up the National Covenant on 28 February 1638. This was the beginning of more that 20 years of strife and warfare. Eventually Charles was beheaded by the English.

The fabric of St Giles has changed little from Jenny's day, but one does not really need an excuse to visit such an intriguing historic edifice. There are tombs of exquisite beauty, such as those of James Graham the Marquis of Montrose and Archibald Campbell, which are situated at opposite sides of the church; both were victims of the unrest created after Jenny's defiant act. And the astonishing woodwork of the Thistle Chapel should not be missed. But today Jenny has her own monument. A three-legged bronze stool, known as a cutty-stool, stands on a wooden plinth in memory of her deed.

As is usual in Scotland, there is an argument over whether she threw a three-legged stool like the one on the monument, or whether it was a folding stool.

I am told the Society of Antiquaries in Scotland had in its collection the cutty-stool that Jenny actually threw, but another account states that Jenny threw her cutty-stool and creels into a great bonfire lit in Edinburgh to celebrate the Restoration of Charles II in 1660, the supposed year of her death.

One wee piece of trivia that intrigues is the fact that in 1787, in Edinburgh, Robert Burns bought for four pounds a trusty horse that he was to use on his travels round Scotland. He named this mare Jenny Geddes.

CHAPTER 21
Jenny Cameron

I FEEL THAT I have a little connection with Jenny Cameron (in some books she is called Jean, and I think the Jenny bit might actually stem from the familiar name for Jean, Jeannie!), as she is buried only a mile or two from my house. I first came across the site of her grave as a boy. I was always one for wandering and exploring, and today it stands in a children's play area. On entering to take advantage of the climbing frame and other assorted amusements, I paused to read the stone that marks the spot. I don't suppose that at that tender age I would ever have imagined that Scottish history would become my passion, but I had a curiosity even then for all things Scottish and that did not seem unusual to me at the time. It was just what I did.

I suppose this chapter is really about two Jenny Camerons, who were contemporaries, but that will be explained as you read on.

The main Jenny of our story was the daughter of a Highland Chieftain, Cameron of Glen Dessary. In 1745, when Prince Charles Edward Stewart landed in Scotland to begin the final struggle to regain the throne for the ancient Stewart dynasty, Jenny was described in the *Lyon in Mourning*, a book written about the '45, as a 'genteel, well-looking, handsome woman, with a pair of pretty eyes and hair as black as jet, of between forty and fifty years of age, of a very sprightly genius and very agreeable in conversation'.

She had been married to an Irish 'gentleman' by the name of O'Neil, but due to his brutal behaviour she had left him and returned to her native Highlands.

There is some debate as to what Jenny's role was at the actual unfurling of the royal standard and the gathering of the Jacobite forces at Glenfinnan. Some accounts say that she led out the Cameron clan and was in charge of some two to three hundred men. But it would seem that the truth of the matter is that she accompanied her brother, Captain Allan Cameron, the leader of the Cameron fighting men, on his journey to Glenfinnan to declare for the prince. She did give a gift of cattle to the prince, but there is no record of her actually being presented personally to him.

Once the ceremony was over she returned to her own lands, where she took control of the Cameron estates and managed them during the entire length of the prince's campaign.

There is a visitor centre and round tower topped with the statue of a clansman at Glenfinnan, and visitors flock there to see where the fateful events of the '45 began, but the actual site of the unfurling of the standard took place several hundred yards away. To find the spot, one must cross to the west bank of the River Finnan by the road bridge and park at the church on the left as you start to climb the hill. On the right-hand side of the road is the old manse, and behind this manse on top of the knoll, there is a carven slab of rock that has a cross marking where the standard actually stood, with the footprints of the main participants also carved into the stone. The whereabouts of this stone had been lost, but a scrub fire in the late 1900s uncovered it to human eyes once more. So it is possible to stand where Prince Charles stood and where the cry went up from the assembled ranks, a shout of welcome to '*Prionnsa Tearlach Righ nan Ghaidheal*' (Prince Charles, King of the Gael), with Jenny among the assembled throng.

You will notice that the Gaelic word for Charles is '*Tearlach*'. The pronunciation of this word sounds very like the English 'Charlie', and so the popular name of 'Bonnie Prince Charlie' actually stems from this.

Propaganda by the press is nothing new; the gutter press in London was quick to name Jenny as Prince Charles' mistress. Pictures were printed, showing her in full highland man's garb, complete with sword and pistols! She was named again and again as Charles' mistress throughout the campaign, and it was stated that she was following in his train. It was reported that she was captured after the Battle of Falkirk, a victory for Charles in January 1746.

This is all somewhat at odds with the fact that she was home in her clan lands managing the Cameron estates.

It seems there may be a reason for this confusion. After Falkirk, while Prince Charles was at Stirling, a Miss Jenny Cameron who owned a milliner's business in Edinburgh heard that a relative was lying wounded in the camp and set out to Stirling to visit him. The Duke of Cumberland, moving the Hanoverian army forward as Charles' army retreated from Stirling, captured this unfortunate woman and when she gave her name, it was assumed she was the famous Jenny whose name had been mentioned so often in the 'British' press.

Cumberland himself wrote to the Duke of Newcastle on 2 February 1746, stating, 'We have taken about 20 of their sick here, and the famous Miss Jenny Cameron, whom I propose to send to Edinburgh for the Lord Justice Clerk to examine, as I fancy she may be a useful evidence against them, if a little threatened.' By his own words, Cumberland lives up to the soubriquet given him by the Scots: 'The Butcher'. A boor of a man, who slaughtered helpless captives and wounded men after the fateful battle at Culloden, it seems he had no qualms about abusing women either.

This Jenny, who was of course innocent of all charges, was incarcerated in Edinburgh Castle. According to the *Scots Magazine* of November 1746, she was kept there till the 15th of that month. When she reopened her shop on her release, the citizens of Edinburgh thronged to her premises, all wishing to buy from the famous Jenny Cameron, lover of a prince. It seems Jenny was happy to go along with this and did not seek to contradict those who made this claim.

There is a report of a Jenny Cameron in very old age in Edinburgh, dressed in the garb of a man, and having a wooden leg, so it seems that the milliner eventually fell on hard times, but that writers were still confusing her with the one who was at Glenfinnan in 1745.

The 'real' Jenny eventually moved to East Kilbride, Lanarkshire, in Scotland's central belt, taking charge of a farm with a fine house at Blacklaw. This farm came to be known as 'Mount Cameron' because of her association with the place and I have heard it called by both names locally. It seems that Jenny was on visiting terms with the local lairds and was well liked by all. She retained her wit and good conversation, and most of all, loved to discuss politics.

William and John Hunter, originally residents of East Kilbride, became famous for their work in, respectively, surgery and biology. William returned to his family home at Long Calderwood in 1751 and he is known to have visited Jenny at Blacklaw. Their birthplace at Long Calderwood is now a museum. The famous Hunterian Museum and Art Gallery at Glasgow University was formed from collections donated by this family.

Jenny attended the parish church of East Kilbride, which I can see from my window. It stands on an ancient site, once having been a druid temple, its old circular graveyard probably reflecting the original outline. When Christianity came to the area through the preaching of St Bride, who gave the town its name, the old temple was the place he chose for his monk's cell, so helping to oust the old religion. Several churches later graced the spot. The church was rebuilt in 1777, but retaining vestiges of the earlier building, notably the visibly older stonework in the lower half of the bell tower.

Jenny died on 27 June 1772. It is reported that her last wish was that her body be taken north, to be buried in Lochaber. This wish was not carried out, and she was buried in a little clump of trees near her house. The trees were eventually cut down and her grave became part of a field that was regularly ploughed.

Stories began to circulate that Mount Cameron House was haunted because Jenny's last wish to be buried in Lochaber had not been carried out. One resident of a nearby farm cottage called Muckethill swore that he had seen a burning cross hovering above her grave. Like so many famous Scots, it seems Jenny was not destined to lie in peace. About the year 1820, Blacklaw was owned by a farmer of the name of Pollock. It had been rumoured that Jenny had been buried with expensive rings on her fingers, so the sons of the house decided to dig up her body and avail themselves of this 'treasure'. They dug down to the heavy oak coffin, but made such a noise trying to unearth it and break into it, that their mother heard the noise. Berating them, she made sure they returned the coffin to its place and filled in the hole.

East Kilbride was designated a 'New Town' in 1947 to deal with the surplus population overspill of Glasgow, and the once quiet farming village was to expand hugely. Jenny's grave was surrounded by the modern suburb of St Leonard's, a name that comes from an ancient leper hospital which once stood near the bridge over the River Calder at Newhousemill, where a stone marks the spot. St Leonard, also known as St Lazarus, was the patron saint of lepers.

Jenny's house, Blacklaw, was demolished in 1958. I do wish historic old places like this had been preserved, even if to be divided into apartments. I'm sure people would have liked to have lived in a building with such a good story attached to it.

A tree was planted behind her grave in commemoration and a stone erected to mark the spot. The play area stands in a road named Glen Dessary in memory of her birthplace. There are streets with the names of Blacklaw Drive and Mount Cameron Drive in the town named for her too, and the nearby primary school is named Mount Cameron, with the name also posted in the Gaelic, *Bun Camshron*.

It's a strange dichotomy to stand among modern housing and look down at the grave of a woman who watched as one of the most famous events in Scottish history, the Raising of the Standard at Glenfinnan, took place. Kids play, probably oblivious to the proximity of the grave of a woman who watched Prince Charles Edward Stuart, the heir to a line which had governed Scotland since the dawn of time, the descendent of Kenneth MacAlpine, of Robert the Bruce, of Mary Queen of Scots, stand proud as his banner was unfurled. There may be the odd kid, who, like me, read this stone at a tender age and was determined to find out more.

CHAPTER 22
The Maid at Balhaldie

ON BONNIE PRINCE CHARLIE'S march south with his army in 1745 he took up the offer of hospitality from one of his supporters, a well-known Jacobite named MacGregor of Balhaldie.

The name Balhaldie is an area of land by the A9, the major trunk road north that runs close to Dunblane. There is still a farm by the name of Balhaldie by the petrol station on the A9 a mile or two north of Dunblane, on the southbound side.

MacGregor of Balhaldie also owned a townhouse in Dunblane, Balhaldie House, which still stands gable-end on to the High Street, at the junction with Smithy Loan. This house has a plaque on its street-facing gable wall, announcing its historical connection to Charlie. It states:

> Balhaldie House late 17th century. The town house of Alexander Drummond or MacGregor of Balhaldie, a notable Jacobite. Prince Charles Edward Stuart stayed here on the night of the 11th and 12th September, 1745.

The prince and his army marched on to Derby, where false propaganda informed them that they were faced with three separate armies and the fateful decision was made to retreat to Scotland. In charge of this pursuit was the Duke of Cumberland, son of the Hanoverian King George. On the route north Charles slept in most of the same beds he had slept in on the journey south. In a strange twist, Cumberland always insisted on sleeping in the same bed that Charles had slept in the night before. What he gained from this is anybody's guess!

Back in Scotland in early 1746, Cumberland was heading north, the day of the fateful Battle of Culloden growing close, the end of Stuart hopes to regain their throne soon to be dashed.

Charles had again been in residence at Balhaldie; Cumberland turned up on 5 February to occupy the Prince's bed. One of the maidservants, whose name unfortunately has not been handed down to us, hit upon a ruse to do away with the Anglo-Germanic Cumberland once and for all.

Knowing he was approaching the house, she heated up a pan of water till it began to seethe and boil. She waited till Cumberland was riding beneath an upper window and tipped the boiling contents onto his head, hoping, at the least, to scald him badly. As you can imagine, all hell broke loose. The maid escaped by a back door and made her getaway, using a small stream that ran down into the Allan Water for cover. It seems Cumberland escaped serious injury.

In memory of this girl, there is a circular plaque dedicated to her on the side wall of Dunblane's Bank of Scotland. It reads:

> MINNIE BURN. Near this spot in a 'cundie' or stone channel, flows the Minnie Burn. It was used as an escape route for a maidservant of Balhaldie House, who on 5 February 1746 attempted to murder the Duke of Cumberland by pouring boiling water on his head from an upper window as he rode by in pursuit of the Jacobite army. She was never caught!

No matter your feelings towards the Jacobite army of Bonnie Prince Charlie and his claim to the throne, I can never forgive the actions of Cumberland and his slaughter of Scots. He well deserves his nickname, the 'Butcher' Cumberland. Prince Charles was magnanimous in his treatment of prisoners, but Cumberland had Scots hung and disembowelled, and one was even skinned.

My sympathies lie with the unknown maidservant. I only wish her aim – and luck – had been better!

CHAPTER 23
Clementina Walkinshaw

CLEMENTINA WAS BORN in 1720 into a well-heeled Glasgow family. She is said to be the youngest of 10 girls. Her father, John Walkinshaw, was a noted Jacobite, one of those who wished the return of a monarch with the blood of the ancient Kings of Scots flowing in his veins. But he could never have anticipated that the twists and turns of fate would eventually mean his daughter would become the mistress – some say wife – of the man whose veins bore that royal blood, Prince Charles Edward Stuart, Bonnie Prince Charlie, as he is commonly known to Scots.

John Walkinshaw, like many of the city's businessmen in that era, made his money in the blossoming trade with North America, Glasgow being the quickest European port to reach from America's eastern seaboard. He owned the estates of Barrowfield and Camlachie, then open countryside to the east of Glasgow, now both the names of not terribly salubrious housing schemes near Parkhead, the home of Celtic Football Club. John Walkinshaw founded the weaving village of Calton, now also enveloped by city sprawl. But that village has become famous in song and history for the exploits and fate of its weavers.

Clementina was most likely born at the large house at Camlachie, but a house in Glasgow's Gallowgate, which survived till the late 1800s, was sometimes pointed out by locals as her birthplace. Some say she was born in Rome.

The story of Clementina and her prince is the stuff of fairy-tale. It runs like this.

John Walkinshaw had fought for the Jacobite forces at the Battle of Sheriffmuir in 1715. There are several memorial stones to this battle at its site on a shoulder of the Ochil Hills. He was taken prisoner and confined in Stirling Castle, but managed to escape to the continent. He was accredited in helping aid the escape of Queen Clementina Sobieski, mother of Prince Charles Edward, from Innsbruck where she had been arrested by the Holy Roman Emperor en route to marry Charles' father, the *de jure* King of Scots, James VIII. It is said that this had been done with the connivance of George of Hanover, who feared the threat that children of this marriage would create to his keeping the throne of England. Then the story goes that when John was joined in Rome by his wife, she bore him a child. The queen, in gratitude for his chivalrous behaviour, was godmother to the daughter named in her honour. This may be a romantic addition, though it is not impossible that it is the truth of the matter.

Clementina's mother, Catherine Paterson, came from an illustrious Jacobite family – her father was Sir Hugh Paterson of Bannockburn, who resided at Bannockburn House. A strange little quirk is that one of Clementina's sisters, called Catherine after her mother, though brought up in this environment of loyalty to the Stuart cause, had taken service in one of the households of the usurping Hanoverian dynasty. She was on the staff of Frederick, the eldest son of George II, and spent much time at the London palace of Whitehall. It seems Clementina would on occasion, join her sister in London, and so she was, to a certain extent, familiar with court life.

During the Jacobite uprising, known in our history books as the '45, after the year 1745 when Prince Charles landed in Scotland to attempt to reclaim the throne of his ancestors, Charles' army had reached Derby when rumours of overwhelming odds stacked against them forced the decision to return to Scottish soil. When he reached Glasgow on 26 December, Charles took up residence in Shawfield House, an imposing residence in the city's Argyle Street, at the junction of Glassford Street. There is a plaque on the baronial building close to where it stood, testifying the fact that Charles stayed there. Shawfield House had extensive gardens that ran down the route of Glassford Street, to where the city's Italian Centre stands today.

Clementina was one of several attractive Jacobite ladies who attended Charles during his stay. It seems that there was an immediate spark between them. A week or so later, Charles moved his army to the area surrounding Stirling and took up residence at Bannockburn House, with which, of course, Clementina had a family connection. It seems she joined him there. In a letter written in Boulogne in 1750, she states that 'between 1745 and 1747' she was 'undone'. We can infer from this that her intimate involvement with the Prince began at Bannockburn House. (It looks today much as it would have done during Charles' sojourn, although apparently it bore a white harling back in early 1746. It stands close to the roundabout at the Stirling/Bannockburn turn-off with its service area, on the M8 and M9 motorways, its entrance on the road to Bannockburn village. It is a private property.)

The Jacobite army continued the march north, and Charles' ambitions came to an end on the heath of Drummossie Muir on 16 April 1746 at the Battle of Culloden, where the loyal clans were slaughtered and the hoped for restoration of the Stuart dynasty came to a conclusion. After the battle Charles wandered the Highlands looking for a way to escape to the continent and avoiding the red-coated government troops scouring the countryside in the hope of capturing him. A huge reward was put on his head, but loyal Highlanders helped him elude his pursuers for several months till he was able to make his way back to France.

At some point between 1750 and 1752 Clementina arrived in Flanders, where she joined a Chapter of Canonesses. Whether she was there by Charles' invitation is unknown, but it was not long until word was brought to Charles, at that time residing in not too distant Ghent, regarding her whereabouts. He asked one of his envoys to arrange a meeting with her in Paris but the envoy declined, telling Charles that such a commission was 'only for the worst of men'.

Nonetheless, the two were soon reunited and at first seemed to coexist happily enough. They moved from Paris to Liège, where, in 1753, Clementina bore Charles a daughter who was named Charlotte. There is a story that Clementina had already borne Charles a son who died as a small infant, but I cannot substantiate this and the timescale would seem to be too short for such an occurrence to have taken place. Charlotte was baptised in the parish church of Nôtre Dame aux Fonts, which, as its name suggests, was the baptistery of the city, now in modern Belgium. This church stood in the shadow of the cathedral of Nôtre Dame et Saint Lambert. Liège, a city-state, was soon to be incorporated within the expanding borders of France. During the French Revolution of 1789 both of the above churches were destroyed, but concerned individuals managed to secrete the early 12th-century baptismal font from which the smaller church took its name and it is today on show in the city's St Bartholomew's Church. So the font in which Charlotte was baptised has survived.

As there was now an heir, stories began to spread that Charles and Clementina had been secretly married and that Charlotte was legitimate, and so was rightful heiress to the throne of Scotland – and England too, for that matter. But Clementina insisted that Charlotte should be raised in the Roman Catholic faith and this caused a strong difference of opinion between mother and father. Charles had secretly visited London in 1750, where his stay, in Exeter Street, is commemorated by a plaque. While there he converted to the Anglican faith at the church of St Mary's le Strand. He believed that Charlotte being raised in the Catholic faith would bar her from any future claim to the throne. Clementina left Charles, but it was not long till they were reunited. Charles was growing more dependent on what his brother Henry called the 'nasty bottle' and it seems his conduct towards Clementina became increasingly violent. Matters were not helped by the fact that his followers were suspicious of her, some thinking she was a spy. Others were worried by the fact that Charles could not marry a suitable bride as long as he was with her. You can read between the lines and see that Charles did indeed care for Clementina, but theirs was a volatile, destructive relationship. Matters came to a head in 1760 when she left him for good. They were never to see each other again, though Charles asked her several times to reconsider, and bring their daughter with her. It seems he swung between desperately missing his daughter and refusing to support her in any way. But Charlotte would return, to nurse her father during his final few years of life.

Clementina, who later became known as the Countess of Albestroff, outlived both Charles, who died in January 1788, and her daughter, who died in November 1789. Clementina lived into the next century, dying in 1802 in Switzerland.

CHAPTER 24
Charlotte, Duchess of Albany

THE STORY OF the only surviving child of the liaison between Prince Charles Edward Stuart of Scotland and Clementina also explains the conclusion of the true royal line of Scotland. Charlotte, born illegitimately on 29 October 1753, was raised at her mother's insistence in the Roman Catholic faith. This, coupled with Charles' increasingly violent behaviour and heavy drinking, meant her parents went their separate ways in 1760. Charlotte was raised in various French convents. Her father did not put aside any provision for her and as she grew into womanhood, refused her permission to marry.

Charlotte continually sent pleading letters to her father, asking for his help for herself and her mother, but Charles took no notice. But her grandfather, the *de jure* James VIII of Scotland, paid money to allow them to survive in a little style.

Around the age of 22 Charlotte took a lover, Ferdinand de Rohan, the Archbishop of Bordeaux and Cambrai. He had three lines of European royal blood in his veins, but obviously, as archbishop, he was unable to marry. This relationship was kept very secret due to the circumstances of the two participants, but Charlotte bore him three children: Marie (1779), Charlotte (1780) and Charles Edward (1784). Their grandfather, Prince Charles, was unaware of their existence.

Charlotte joined Charles at the Palazzo Muti in Rome in 1784 for the last three years of his life and nursed him, probably trying hard to keep him away from alcohol. It seems he had degenerated badly. Charles had her legitimised, bestowing upon her the right to be known as 'Her Royal Highness', and she was gifted the title 'Duchess of Albany', by which she is best known. Albany is an ancient Scottish title, based on the Gaelic word for Scotland, 'Alba'.

During this period, Charlotte's three children remained with Clementina. Charlotte was not in the best of health herself. She had a liver problem that some say was brought on by a fall from a horse.

There are records of her having her clothing altered to cover the growth that this problem was causing. Her father had a fatal stroke and died on 31 January 1788. Strangely, he was born and died in the same building, the Palazzo Muti, which still stands in Rome's Piazza del Santa Apostoli. It is not open to the public, but there are plaques announcing its Stuart connection in the carriage entrance-way at the front of the building.

The street takes its name from the ancient Church of the Apostles which stands at a right angle to the palace. This church, visited by Charles and Charlotte, has one of the most stunningly beautiful interiors of any building on the planet. I've been lucky to have visited it a few times and I always pause just within the door and gaze in awe at that painted ceiling. Are men really capable of creating such things? The heart of Charles mother, Clementina Sobieski, enclosed in a casket, is set into one of the church pillars with a plaque announcing the fact. The rest of her body is buried in St Peter's Basilica in the Vatican.

Charles was buried at Frascati, where his brother Henry was cardinal, but his body was later moved to St Peter's, where he shares a stone coffin with his brother and father in the crypt where the Popes are buried. There is a large marble monument to these last Stuart 'claimants' at floor level above. Charles' heart was left at Frascati. It is enclosed in an urn that stands under the funerary monument to him there.

Charlotte did not long outlive her father. In Bologna, only 22 months later, on 17 November 1789, she succumbed to her liver ailment and was buried in the church of San Biagio. After this church was pulled down by the French in 1789, her remains were transferred to the city's Oratorio della Santissima Trinita; when this building closed in 1961, her monument and, it is hoped, her remains, were transferred to the nearby Chiesa della Santissima Trinita.

What of Charlotte's children? The youngest, Charles Edward, adopted the title Count Roehenstart (from his father's Rohan, coupled with Stuart). Educated by his father's family in Germany, he became an officer in the Russian Army, then a general in the Austrian army. He visited America and Asia, and as fate would have it, ended up living in Scotland. He died after a coach accident near Stirling Castle and was buried at the very ancient Dunkeld Cathedral, north of Perth, in cathedral grounds bordered by the picturesque River Tay. Jacobite sympathisers often lay wreaths to his memory.

Strangely, it is only in recent years that much detail of this man's life has surfaced. Apparently, when he told folk who he was, Scots just thought he was telling tall tales, especially where stories of his royal descent were told!

He died without fathering children.

Of the two girls, Marie ended up in Poland after the French Revolution. She married a wealthy Polish nobleman who was also a banker and bore him a son, Antime. Her younger sister died childless. There are people today who can claim a direct descent from Antime and so bear the ancient bloodline of Scotland; various books have been written laying claim to this blood-line.

Charlotte never visited Scotland, the land from which her blood-line sprang. But she has one little connection with Scotland, and that is the fact that Robert Burns dedicated a poem to her, scorning the Hanoverian dynasty:

> My heart is wae, and unco wae,
> To think upon the raging sea,
> That roars between her gardens green,
> An' th' bonnie lass of ALBANIE. –
>
> This lovely maid's of nobel blood,
> That ruled Albion's kingdoms three;
> But Oh, Alas! for her bonie face,
> They hae wrang'd the lass of ALBANIE.
>
> In the rolling tide of spreading Clyde,
> There sits an isle of high degree,
> And a town of fame whose princely name,
> Should grace the lass of ALBANIE.
>
> But there's a youth, a witless youth,
> That fills the place where she should be;

We'll send him o'er to his native shore,
And bring our ain sweet ALBANIE.

Alas the day, and woe the day,
A false Usurper wan the gree,
Who now commands the towers and lands –
The royal right of ALBANIE.

We'll daily pray, we'll nightly pray,
On bended knees most fervently,
That the time may come, with pipe an' drum,
We'll welcome hame fair ALBANIE.

CHAPTER 25
The Finsthwaite Princess

WHEN I FIRST thought of writing this book, I wanted to include quirky stories about some of the lesser-known women of Scotland's history. This next story is not only quirky, but also interesting too, I hope.

Perhaps it should not be a surprise how little-known the Finsthwaite Princess is in Scotland, as this story is set in the Lake District in the northwest of England. To Scottish ears, Finsthwaite is a name that sounds incredibly Anglo-Saxon, though I believe that it is a corruption of the old Norse word for meadow, 'thveit'; so Finsthwaite is likely to mean simply 'Finns meadow'.

Finsthwaite, a picturesque little village just southwest of Lake Windermere, is not much more than a few houses clustered close to its unusual church, which, for its size, has quite a heavy squat tower and spire. It comes under the auspices of the ancient Carmel Priory, in the village of Carmel to the south; that early medieval building also has a squat tower, though without a spire, so it seems to be the local style. The church in Finsthwaite is of fairly recent construction, built between 1874 and 1875 to replace an older building dating from 1724.

The thing that elicits our interest though, is a grave in the churchyard: a simple stone cross on a little plinth, bearing the inscription: 'Clementina Johannes Sobiesky Douglass of Waterside. In memoriam, buried 16th day of May 1771'.

From previous chapters it should be clear why this is of interest, the name Sobieski (though it is spelt with a 'Y' on the inscription) is that of the great royal dynasty of Poland, and the surname of the Queen of James VIII and mother of Prince Charles Edward Stuart. The plot thickens when we see the unusual name of Clementina too, as Clementina Walkinshaw was named after Clementina Sobieski. It does not seem to be a very common name for the 1700s, other than the odd use by Jacobite sympathisers. The local story is that Clementina Walkinshaw bore a child to Prince Charles (as she did, of course, in the shape of Charlotte, Duchess of Albany), and that this other child named Clementina after her mother, was sent to the 'backwater' of Finsthwaite to be raised in relative obscurity.

Another version, one that is more probable, is that Charles, when marching through the area with his army – which he did twice, on the way south to Derby, then on the return north – he and his men followed the line of what is now the A6 north–south route – had a dalliance with a local girl, and the child born from this liaison became known as the Finsthwaite Princess. He certainly spent the night at the not too distant town of Kendal, where he stayed at Stricklandgate House, today a little art gallery and coffee house with a plaque announcing its 'Charlie' connection at the front door.

That the princess actually lived and was not just a figment of imagination would seem to be without doubt, as on 28 April 1770, she witnessed and signed the will of her landlord at Waterside.

The tale has grown arms and legs over the years. During the Second World War a story circulated that the War Office took a certain interest in the grave, and that the future Duke of Edinburgh, Philip, was seen visiting it – the supposed reason being that the Germans, if they invaded, might seek to somehow use the princess to topple the Windsor/Hanoverian dynasty from the throne. Nonsense, of course.

There are other tales of a pleat of blond hair being discovered, that her tomb had been opened for some reason and a length of blue ribbon found within. Why a piece of blue ribbon should be imbued with such an air of mystery I have no idea, but when I hear the story told this blue ribbon is often mentioned as if it has a major bearing on the truth of the matter!

What adds to the mystery is that Prince Charles did indeed use the pseudonym Douglas on occasion, although the Princess's surname has a double 's' on the inscription.

The first time I visited her grave was around 2004, when I, along with a few carloads of acquaintances, drove to Finsthwaite to pay our respects to this lady who was said to be of the Scottish royal line. We aroused the attention of some of the villagers as we wandered round the churchyard in full original Highland dress, bagpipes playing, all armed to the teeth! A wreath was laid at her grave and my friend Kenny let rip with his musket in salute, causing a few locals, unused to the effects of black powder, to jump.

There is another line of inscription on her gravestone: 'Behold thy Kingdom Cometh'. Very much double-edged, with its Biblical connotations, and the legend that this girl was of the royal line of Scotland, and that one day that throne would again be in the hands of the Stuarts.

Finsthwaite does not stand at too great a distance west from the modern M6 motorway; a visit can be coupled with a visit to Cartmel Priory and the gaunt ruins of Furness Abbey near the town of Barrow-in-Furness. James the Good, the Black Douglas, visited both these places. But he was here to exact tribute, in exchange for immunity from burning by the Scots, that helped to fund the war against England. The Princess, whoever she was, seemed to be looked upon by the locals with a more friendly aspect, notwithstanding the fact that she used a similar surname. Though I should point out that the claims of her identity make her a direct descendent of Robert the Bruce, under whose instructions the Douglas operated!

CHAPTER 26
Mary Slessor

MANY PEOPLE IN Scotland look upon an image of Mary Slessor on an almost daily basis, as hers is the face that currently graces Clydesdale Bank ten pound notes. I suppose some have no idea who she was. A few know that she was a missionary working in Africa. When you look into her story, you will have no doubt that she was a Scotswoman, with all the associated traits – compassion and fiery temper rolled into one.

Mary was born in Gilcomston, a suburb of Aberdeen, on 2 December 1848. She was a blue-eyed, red-haired girl and she had the determination and attitude that Scots often associate with that hair colouring.

When Mary was 10 her family moved to Dundee. Her father, Robert, was a shoemaker to trade, but he had an alcohol dependency and perhaps because of this problem abandoned his trade and became a mill labourer. Her mother, an extremely pious woman who had a particular fascination with missionary work in Africa, did her best for Mary in difficult circumstances. At the age of 11 Mary was given employment in a jute mill as a 'half-timer' – for half of the day she received schooling, while the other half was spent weaving jute. Jute grown in the Indian sub-continent was exported to Europe and Dundee became the centre of the jute-spinning industry, the manufacture of sacks, packaging, backing for carpets and the like. When Mary began her working life, jute was entering its 'glory years': 50,000 people were employed in 60 factories spread across the city. It was arduous, unhealthy work, and jute workers' home conditions were often inadequate and insanitary.

Mary, like her mother, was a member of the congregation of Dundee's Wishart Church. The church was named after George Wishart, a protestant preacher who was active in Scotland in the 1500s.

By the time Mary was 14 she was full-time at the mill, rising at 5am and working from 6am till 6pm, already regarded as a skilled jute worker. Although her education at the mill had finished, she had absorbed all that she could. And I'm sure older girls working alongside her forwarded her education in other ways. Mary was probably feisty enough to deal with real problems in the real world in no uncertain way.

When a mission opened in Quarry Pend, near the Wishart Church, she asked to become a teacher there. She wanted to carry religion to the locals. A gang tried to intimidate her, saying that they would swing a weight on a string closer and closer to her face. Mary struck a deal, that if she did not flinch, they had to join her mission as a forfeit. The weight was indeed swung and Mary stood her ground, not changing her stance or expression. She won her bet. This grit was to stand her in good stead throughout her life.

Mary was fascinated by the stories of the missionaries working in Africa and hoped to follow in their footsteps, but she doubted her own abilities, describing herself as 'wee and thin and not very strong'. There are different types of strength and Mary had personality enough to counteract any lack of physical strength. Notwithstanding her small physical stature, she eventually applied to the Foreign Mission section of the united Presbyterian Church, asking if she could dedicate her life in the service of the tribes of the Calabar region, part of modern-day Nigeria. The Scots missionary David Livingstone had blazed a path in this type of work, and Mary must have wondered whether she could live up to the standards he had set.

After a period of training in Edinburgh, at the age of 28, Mary set sail on the SS *Ethiopia* on 5 August 1876. It took a month to reach West Africa. She travelled inland to Calabar, through sweltering countryside utterly different from anything she had experienced before. Mosquitoes and malaria were rife. In the following years she was to suffer illness many times, but she never desisted from her quest. She managed to shrug off the ill effects time and time again, though disease did debilitate many other European missionaries for the rest of their lives.

The wild landscape teemed with dangerous animals and insects, and the tribesmen were armed to the teeth and thought nothing of taking a human life. On the death of a chief, human sacrifice was carried out to appease the Gods. Women were the lowest of the low, with no rights whatsoever. When twins were born they were either slain or cast into the forest, due to the superstition that during conception an evil spirit had created one of the children.

Mary made it her life's work to put an end to these horrors once and for all, and this little redhead with her Scottish temperament was not about to let anyone stand in her way. She decided to dress to suit the climate, and discarded the hats, heavy dresses and corsets that 'society' expected her to wear. She wore light and airy dresses, eminently sensible in that heat, and started to learn Efik, the local language. She knew that if she wished to argue her case and influence the tribespeople, it was best to speak to them in their own language. She eventually became fluent. Recordings of Mary speaking in this language have survived! When you realise that you can hear this woman actually speak, you realise that hers is not a story of antiquity, and her work is from fairly recent history.

Anecdotes of Mary are legion. Once when confronted with some fearsome warriors, she dispersed them with her umbrella, whacking about her for all she was worth. On another occasion she stepped into a tribal argument. One chief had many wives, and two of these wives, only 16 years old, had crept out in the night from his hut, where they were expected to remain, and were discovered in the hut of a young man. It was decreed that the young man had bewitched them, but witchcraft notwithstanding, they were all sentenced to one hundred lashes; salt would be rubbed into the wounds and mutilation may have also been involved. This was basically a death sentence, as each stroke of the lash would lift a strip of skin. Mary argued long and hard, speaking to the elders in their own tongue. She may have been a Christian missionary, but she was not blinded by the Victorian morality of her time and had a broad-minded outlook. She told the elders: 'It is a disgrace to you and a cruel injustice to these helpless girls. Only 16 years old, full of fun and frolic, yet you shut them up in a hut – it is a blot on your manhood! Obedience to your sort of laws is not worth having!'

Mary managed to get their sentence reduced to 10 lashes each and after the punishment had been meted out she was on hand with ointment and bandages for their wounds.

She was especially horrified at the killing of twins and constantly argued the case for their rights. She adopted some of these children; twins grew up under her supervision and she took many of them with her on her travels, even on one occasion, back to Scotland. Her influence broke the tradition of the killings as she made the people realise that twins were a blessing from God.

She began to live among the tribespeople, ate with them and slept among the women. Although she spoke in broad Scots, she conversed with them in their own tongue, fluent enough to be able to use sarcasm and humour. She was convinced of their need for Christian religion and that their ideas of witchcraft came from fear and lack of understanding. She had a receptive audience who needed some sort of stability in their lives: she offered that stability. She caused churches and schools to be built and a light began to shine in a country where only despair and darkness had been seen before.

Once, during a canoe journey, a great storm arose. A drummer made sure that the rowers kept time, but in his fear he stopped playing and the rowers also stopped, letting the boat be tossed in the turbulent water like a cork. Mary began to shout at the drummer, berating him till he started the beat again. They made it to an island where they were all able to hang onto a mangrove tree for dear life till the storm had passed.

Mary wished to move further inland and work with a tribe of warriors called the Okoyong. Male missionaries had previously visited the Okoyong, but these warlike, muscled warriors had instilled fear into them. They told Mary that she should not go among them.

But go she did. She made several visits and then she was told by the Okoyong that they would allow her to live in their main village. She discovered that just a few weeks before she went to live among them, the tribe had attended a funeral where they had strangled the dead man's four widows, along with eight other men, eight other women and five girls and five boys. Mary was determined to educate the Okoyong and stamp out this behaviour. She set up a church of sorts and began to hold services which became more and more popular. Mary also held her own clinic where she treated people with modern medicine, something previously unknown to these people.

But each and every night, the tribe would drink itself senseless – they made their own alcohol. Mary wrote that she lay down at night, 'knowing that not a sober man and hardly a sober woman was within miles of me'. She reported that drunken orgies took place where slave girls were subjected to the lust of the menfolk.

On one occasion she was defending a young man and trying to save him from a death sentence for a trivial act. She stood her ground so well that the warriors began to brandish spears and threaten her, but she was not to be intimidated and stood, arms folded, glaring back. These men began to listen. Eventually respect for Mary started to permeate the tribes, who knew her as Eka Kpukpro Owo, which literally means 'Mother of all the Peoples'; they often simply referred to her as 'Ma'.

A visiting official reported my own favourite Mary Slessor story. She was sitting in a rocking chair with a baby in her lap, listening to grievances and sorting out disputes. The official recounted:

> She suddenly jumped up with an angry growl, handed the baby to a bystander and she sped to the door where a hulking overdressed native stood. She seized him by the scruff of the neck and boxed his ears and hustled him out into the yard.

It transpired that the man was a local chief who had disobeyed her. He had been banned from attending her 'court' until he apologised, but had not done so.

Mary's faith was steadfast, no matter the odds stacked against her. She wrote into her Bible: 'God and one is a majority'. She remained single, although it is told that she once became engaged to a much younger missionary. But ill health forced him to return home and on doctor's orders he was unable to return to Africa and the engagement was quietly forgotten.

Later in her life roads began to be constructed in the region and Mary could look upon a complete social change, her influence having stamped out the old superstitious ways. Women were no longer the mere chattels they had been before her arrival. The High Commissioner of Nigeria reported that 'Miss Slessor can go where no man can go, she can sway the people when we cannot sway them'.

Right to the end of her days Mary worked her miracles. Even when her health began to fade, she put in a huge daily workload. Near the end, so weak had she become, that this woman who would once have made long treks through hostile jungle terrain had to be pushed along by her friends in a handcart.

She died in January 1915, aged 66, surrounded by the people she loved. She was buried in Calabar. Her grave is marked by a large granite cross projecting from a cairn, very much in the Scottish style. It is in a graveyard on a hilltop, some 200 metres from the University of Calabar Teaching Hospital. It is perhaps fitting that a modern medical facility is within sight of her last resting place.

CHAPTER 27
Elsie Inglis

ELSIE INGLIS' PARENTS were Scottish, but she was born, on 18 August 1864, in India at the Naini Tal Hill Station where her father was serving in the Indian Civil Service. It was the days of the Raj, as the time of the occupation of India under the British Empire was known, and Elsie was born into a very male-dominated society in which women were generally expected to be no more than wives and mothers. She certainly broke that mould.

From an early age Elsie had an interest in medicine and her father did all he could to help her realise her dream of a career in that field. When he retired in 1878 the family returned to Scotland and settled in Edinburgh.

When she was old enough, Elsie enrolled in the Edinburgh School of Medicine for women. That such a facility existed at that time was a miracle in itself. Sophia Jex Blake, a pioneer in this field, had set it up. Although Jex Blake was a noted suffragette, she drew no wages for her work, as it was thought demeaning for women to 'labour', and was supported by her wealthy family instead.

One of the girls in Elsie's class, a Miss Sinclair, failed an exam, but prevailed on the male examination board, and when the circumstances were explained they issued her with a pass certificate. Jex Blake, who, although a wonderful teacher, had a very abrasive attitude, accused Miss Sinclair of dishonourable conduct. I would assume that Jex Blake thought that sexual favours were involved! Elsie became embroiled in the defence of Miss Sinclair and this episode ended with Elsie leaving and with the backing of her father and some wealthy friends, starting her own medical training school in Edinburgh. She also attended classes at Glasgow University, famous the world over for medicine. It seems Elsie wanted to absorb as much as she could where medicine was concerned.

She graduated as a doctor and went south to work in London. She was appalled at the lack of healthcare for women, especially those of the working classes. Husbands would turn up at the hospitals and demand that their wives come home at once to cook and look after the children, even when they were seriously ill – a ridiculous state of affairs.

She returned to Edinburgh in 1894 and with another woman doctor set up a maternity hospital with a facility for midwifery in the High Street. It was known as 'The Hospice'.

Elsie worked so hard, often spending any free time helping patients, that she began to make a name for herself. One man remarked, 'That woman has done more for the folk living between Morrison Street and the High Street than all the ministers in Edinburgh and Scotland ever did for anyone.' It was also said that:

> Some of these poor creatures who would not rouse themselves, judged that the world was against them. Many a time the patient fighting with circumstances needed a sisterly word of cheer which Dr Inglis supplied, and sent the individual heartened and refreshed.

Elsie fought hard her whole life for the suffragette movement, believing in equal rights and votes for women. She was a founder of the Scottish movement and spoke out on behalf of women's rights. She was to see this part of her life's work come to fruition when women over the age of 30 were granted the right to vote, but by this time, in 1917, she was close to the end of her life, and never herself got to exercise the right to vote. Although she had achieved so much, the days of her greatest triumphs had yet to come. Unfortunately it was the outbreak of the First World War that created the situation that brought her the most fame. She set up an organisation called the Scottish Woman's Hospitals for Foreign Service. The aim was to supply field hospitals completely staffed by women for the Allied war effort. This was a huge leap forward, with women proving their worth. There was still much resistance against women working, never mind staffing hospitals close to the front lines, but Elsie was her usual innovative self and was determined to push forward.

The Scottish Woman's Hospitals, or SWH as they were commonly known, wore uniforms trimmed with tartan: they wore tartan epaulettes on their shoulders, with a metal thistle badge as the centrepiece. The organisation was responsible for hospitals in France, Serbia and Russia. Elsie particularly enjoyed working in Serbia. She seemed to manage to deal with the overwhelming numbers of wounded men her hospitals had to deal with, despite the lack of equipment. She could give harsh tongue-lashings to nurses she felt were not pulling their weigh, on occasion reducing them to tears, so she could be a stern taskmistress indeed.

A strange dichotomy was that Elsie was very much one for taking strides forward, but she still retained much of the mindset of the Victorian era. For instance, she would not tolerate any flirting between her nurses and the male patients. One thing that particularly appalled her was the realisation that some of her nurses had begun swearing. Elsie lambasted the whole unit with a tirade about this behaviour. One nurse retorted that they were at the front lines in a horrific war and surely Elsie liked outspoken girls? Elsie replied that she had never been 'so insulted' in her whole life, that:

> because I like the modern healthy out of door girl with her energy and resource and independence I should approve of language that I would not tolerate in a coster, is an impertinence.

The press back home reported on this remarkable woman and her work and Elsie became a household name in Scotland. Many other countries across Europe were not slow in admitting their admiration too. She was actually taken prisoner once when there was a surprise advance by the Germans. She was held captive for a while, and then because of her status as a medical practitioner the Germans eventually released her to Switzerland, a neutral country, from where she was able to travel back to Scotland, where she immediately made plans to return to her field hospitals on the front. She admitted to her sisters she was suffering from cancer, but so guarded was she about discussing it with anyone, that to this day we do not know what form of cancer it was.

The unit she served with was sent home for a refit in late November

1917. Elsie was very weak and having trouble eating. On arrival, she took to her bed and died on 26 November.

When the news spread, there was a general feeling of mourning, quite extraordinary when one considers there had been warfare with such unprecedented carnage for the previous three years. Her coffin was carried down Edinburgh's Princes Street with the crowds deep on the pavements at either side. She lay in state in St Giles Cathedral, where her funeral service was held and she was buried in the Dean Cemetery. *The Scotsman* newspaper reported:

> Widespread sorrow will be felt at the announcement of the death of Dr Elsie Inglis. Her name has been made familiar in connection with beneficent work in many lands. It will take a high place amongst the records of heroic service in the great struggle.

After the war the SWH was disbanded. With what remained of the organisation's funds, a hospital was built: in July 1925 the 20-bed Elsie Inglis Memorial Maternity Hospital was opened; by the time of its closure in 1988 it had 82 beds. 'Born in the Elsie Inglis' was how generations of Edinburgh citizens described themselves, which is the reason that Elsie's name particularly well known in Scotland's capital.

Banks in Scotland do not use a uniform currency like other nations. In the USA there is the dollar, in England there are the pound notes issued by the Bank of England, but in Scotland each bank issues its own legal tender, though all issues are tied in parity with the pound sterling. In 2009 the Clydesdale Bank issued a fifty-pound note bearing a picture of Elsie on the front. The Clydesdale Bank is to be congratulated for using images of famous Scotswomen on their banknotes. It shows how much Elsie deserves to be remembered and will keep her name in people's minds in Scotland for quite a time to come.

CHAPTER 28
Wendy Wood

I REMEMBER HEARING Wendy Wood's name mentioned when I was a child, and as I grew older I would hear more of her exploits and the stunts she pulled off at one time or another. Although I know some thought of her behaviour a little eccentric, if asked who she was and what she represented, folk in Scotland would all reply that she was a 'Scottish Patriot'.

To be remembered as a patriot, someone who loved her country, would probably have been almost enough for Wendy, other than her wish that she would see the day dawn in her own lifetime when Scotland became a full nation state free of foreign interference.

Wendy Wood was born in Kent in England in October 1892. Her birth name was Gwendoline Meacham, but she eventually shortened Gwendoline to 'Wendy', and used her mother's maiden name 'Wood'. Incidentally, a Scotsman, J.M. Barrie, born in Kirriemuir, invented the name Wendy for the heroine of *Peter Pan*, and the name has since become popular.

Wendy Wood's maternal grandfather was a fairly well known sculptor named S.P. Wood, and his brother was a painter by the name of T.P. Wood, so perhaps she felt that taking that name would afford her a little more credibility and she did become a poet and painter of some note. Her birth in England had taken place because her family had been in transit between Scotland and South Africa, where she was raised. Sometimes she was asked about her place of birth and her right to be an ultra-nationalist Scot,. Her retort was, 'One does not have to be a horse to be born in a stable!'

Wendy was always told as a child that Scotland was 'home'. She was regaled with stories about William Wallace and his struggles to set his country free. It seems that she wanted to emulate Wallace and decided to dedicate her life to the fight for Scotland's freedom. In 1913 she toured Scotland in a motorcar with her husband. It must have been an interesting drive on single-lane Highland roads in those early days of that new form of travel! They visited many of the places she had read about, including the National Wallace Monument on the Abbey Craig near Stirling, which cemented her resolve to emulate the great man.

She joined a series of nationalist organisations in Scotland: the Scottish League in 1916, the Home Rule Association in 1918, and then the Scottish National Movement in 1927. In 1928 the Nationalist Party of Scotland was formed from the uniting of several of the parties of which Wendy was a member. This new organisation would eventually metamorphose into the mainstream Scottish National Party we know today.

Public speaking on Scotland's behalf became Wendy's forte. Her first speech was in Inverkeithing Town Hall, where she spoke for 20 minutes. On average throughout her life, she spoke at major events espousing patriotism and self-governance every 10 days or so.

But, come 1931, she decided on a radical change. She did not like the way that the National Party ignored Scotland's youth, for example, and formed a movement named Scottish Watch. It was a little like the Boy Scout Movement, but not male-only. As a child in South Africa Wendy had become the first female member of the Boy Scout movement there! She obviously drew on that experience to create an organisation that would attract young Scots. At meetings the boys and girls were instructed in tales of Scotland's history, culture and folklore. There were Scottish cookery lessons, the organisation had its own tartan and its own pipers. Scottish Watch were famous for their Scottish Country Dancing lessons, which sometimes were held outdoors: the participants would fill Edinburgh's Royal Mile or Princes Street Gardens, pulling bystanders in to swell the ranks and join the fun.

In 1932, during the annual Bannockburn Day parade, a commemoration of the famous 1314 victory that still goes on to this day, Wendy decided that the Union Flag flying above Stirling Castle was an insult. With a group of followers, she 'stormed' the place, ignoring soldiers with fixed bayonets, and the Union Flag was torn down and replaced by the Lion Rampant, the ancient Royal Standard of Scotland. It seems the soldiers were true Scots, and were loath to actually stand in her way. Ten years after this event, the quartermaster sergeant of the Argylls, the regiment that garrisoned the castle, told Wendy he had the flag she had raised in safekeeping and that it would be flown on the 'right day' – meaning the day that Scotland regained its freedom.

Compton Mackenzie wrote that Wendy had later flushed the purloined Union Flag down a toilet. Wendy took exception to this and sued the author for libel, but in a somewhat humorous ending, she settled out of court for a farthing in damages. (A farthing was worth a quarter of an old style penny, so in today's decimal coinage in Scotland, it is about an eighth of a modern penny.)

Wendy went to prison for her beliefs. She had disrupted a meeting of the Blackshirts, a 1930s fascist organisation, at the Mound in Edinburgh, and was arrested for a possible breach of the peace. While in Saughton Prison, she reached the conclusion that the conditions female prisoners were kept under were unacceptable and resolved to do something about it.

National Insurance is something that all people in Scotland have to pay, and usually it is deducted direct from wages. The headquarters of this institution were moved from Edinburgh to Newcastle in northern England, so Wendy refused to pay her National Insurance. She was charged with the offence, and the judge told her she could pay a £15 fine, or spend 60 days in prison. As you would expect, many of her friends and admirers sent her cheques, but Wendy refused them all and returned them, and so was sent to the well past its sell-by-date, Duke Street Women's Prison in Glasgow. Having gained first-hand experience of prison conditions there, on her release she was able to argue her case and she eventually heard that the Prison Commissioners were going to demolish Duke Street Prison and build a more modern facility in Greenock.

On another occasion she was found guilty of inciting the crowd of Scotland football supporters gathered in London's Trafalgar Square before the 1951 Scotland/England derby match. She was fined five pounds and again refused to pay. The police treated Wendy so roughly because of her known stance on Scottish independence that she began her term in Holloway Prison as a patient in the prison hospital.

Wendy formed an organisation called the Scottish Patriots in 1949 and this group went from strength to strength, at one point having 2,000 members.

When Elizabeth Windsor was crowned, she assumed the title Queen Elizabeth II of Great Britain. There had been a queen of that name in England, the Elizabeth the First from the time of the Spanish Armada and Sir Francis Drake – and who was responsible for the murder by beheading of Mary Queen of Scots. But there had not been a regnant Queen Elizabeth of Scots. Many people in Scotland took exception to the assumption of this title. With her usual aplomb, Wendy decided to do something about it, and was vocal in her condemnation. Some Scots actually blew up a couple of pillar-boxes, as these Royal Mail post boxes carried the moniker ER II in Scotland, the letters standing for 'Elizabeth Regina'.

When Kay Matheson and her colleagues liberated the Stone of Destiny in 1950, there was a strong suspicion by the authorities that Wendy had had a hand in the events. Certainly at a prior date, assisted by her supporters, she had made an attempt to carry off to Scotland the old English Crowning Stone kept at Kingston on Thames (hence the name), in a retaliatory raid for the Scots' Stone being kept at Westminster. She did have a small involvement when the Stone of Destiny was returned to Arbroath Abbey, but she was against this move, as she had an inkling that the Stone would be immediately taken back down south. She was correct in her fears.

In 1960 Wendy addressed the General Assembly of the Church of Scotland. This was highly unusual, women not usually being requested to speak there at that time. She tried to mobilise them into reconvening Scotland's Parliament, which had last met in 1707, arguing that it was merely adjourned, not dissolved. A bold move, but it was not to be carried out.

One of my particular favourite Wendy Wood stories is the moving of the signs that welcome one to Scotland on the main east coast route. Berwick upon Tweed is a Scottish town, standing as it does on the north shore of the mouth of the River Tweed, which marks the border between Scotland and England. But the border line on maps takes a strange twist north round the town, as England claims it for its own due to the fact it stormed and took the town during the old days of warfare. The signs stand some three miles north of the town, on the A1, but Wendy was responsible for having them uprooted and placed in the middle of the bridge over the Tweed. Two of her cohorts were caught and arrested, Donny Paton and Tom Cavanagh. When they appeared before the judge, they would neither speak to him nor acknowledge him. They refused to recognise this English court on Scottish soil, but when Wendy appeared they both stood and saluted her!

In later life Wendy went on hunger strike to get Scotland's case for independence recognised. She was also the author of many books, the last of which, her autobiography, was released in 1970, pertinently titled *Yours Sincerely for Scotland*.

She received a decoration from France for her services to Scotland, the Commander Companionette of the Order of St Lazarus of Jerusalem; a letter, sent to her from Switzerland, addressed simply 'To the famous Madame Wendy Wood, Scotland', arrived safely! A nice touch.

Wendy died in June 1981. I wish she had seen constitutional change for her beloved country, but it would be another 16 years before the Scots would get the chance to have an unrigged vote to have a parliament of their own again. But her example is there as a shining beacon to show that an ordinary girl with a simple love for her country could lead and inspire and leave a legacy of stories to be told to future generations. I know. I was one of them.

As I pass certain places in Scotland, my mind is drawn to people I associate with them. I have never crossed the Royal Tweed Bridge, built at Berwick in 1928 to carry what was known as the Great North Road, without thinking about Wendy Wood, a lady who said 'no' when too many others in Scotland seemed complacent about their political lot.

CHAPTER 29
Kay Matheson

BORN CATRIONA MATHESON in 1928, at Inverasdale by Loch Ewe, near the village of Poolewe in the northwest Highlands, Kay worked as a schoolteacher but is best known for the part she played in the liberation of Scotland's Stone of Destiny from Westminster Abbey in December 1950.

While in Glasgow training as a teacher, Kay joined the Scottish Covenant Association. The National Covenant had been drawn up to put pressure on the London government to recognise Scotland's right to home rule. Eventually it bore two million signatures, an impressive amount given that there are only five million people living in Scotland. She made the acquaintance of fellow members Ian Hamilton, Gavin Vernon and Alan Stuart. Ian wanted to do something radical to shake and wake patriotic fervour in the Scots. He devised a plan to liberate the famed Stone of Destiny, the talisman of the Scottish people. This was the crowning chair of the Kings of Scots, fabled to be Jacob's Pillow from the Bible. It had been looted from Scone in Scotland by King Edward I of England, and taken to Westminster Abbey in London, where it was installed in a Coronation Chair that was specially created for the purpose, so that England could incorporate it into their coronation rituals and symbolically keep Scotland subservient in the process.

The Scots people had long been indignant at this situation, and many times plans to try and return it to its rightful home had been hatched, without success. But that was to change on Christmas Day 1950. Using two old Ford cars, each only 8 horsepower, the four made their way down to London, a journey that took 18 hours in those pre-motorway days.

There was an attempt on Christmas Eve to take the Stone, but it came to naught after Ian Hamilton, who had hidden in the abbey after closing time, was discovered and ejected. The following night, though, he used a jemmy to prise open a side door and he, Gavin Vernon and

Alan Stuart managed to slide the 336 lb Stone from the Coronation Chair. Unfortunately a corner broke off in the process. It was decided to place this broken corner piece into Kay's car – Kay had been keeping watch outside. At one point a policeman came over to ask why the car was parked there. By that time Ian was in the car, and he and Kay went into a clinch and pretended they were a courting couple. The policeman believed their story.

It was decided that Kay should make a getaway with her piece of the Stone. The other three would essay to get the rest of the Stone away and hopefully the two pieces would be reunited back in Scotland.

Kay took her piece to the English Midlands, to be left with trusted friends; Hamilton, Vernon and Stuart managed to secrete the bulk of the Stone in a field in Kent, with the intention of collecting it when the 'heat' died down.

The next day people in Scotland woke to the astonishing news that the Stone had gone from Westminster. There was wild jubilation, everyone sensing that Scots had carried out this audacious raid to take the Stone home.

In reality it had not been straightforward and the series of events was more like the script for a farce in places. When it was over, it seems that the four could hardly believe that they had carried off this daring heist.

The late, great Scottish writer Nigel Tranter told me that he woke the following morning and saw out of his kitchen window the local policeman having a look at his garden over the wall. Nigel was known for his pro-Scottish stance and he had been involved in the National Covenant. Nonplussed, he went out and asked what the problem might be. The policeman casually informed him that he was 'just having a look at your rockery'. It was only when the papers with their burning headlines appeared that the penny dropped for Nigel – and that he had been given a wee 'warning'.

The English establishment was outraged, which only added to the Scots enthusiasm for the unknown perpetrators. Eventually both pieces of the Stone were returned to Scotland, where a patriotic stonemason carried out the repairs to unite them. A hunt was carried out to find who was responsible for rocking English sensibilities. But the Stone had not been brought back to be hidden away and it was decided to bring it out into the open by leaving it at the High Altar of Arbroath Abbey, the place where that striking document of Scotland's independence was created back in 1320.

In April 1951 the authorities arrived at Arbroath to whisk the Stone back to England. Kay was questioned about her involvement, as were the other three, but charges were never brought. The authorities feared the reaction of the Scots people if punishment was meted out. How can you be charged with theft for stealing something that already belongs to you? It would have been a nightmare for the courts.

After the affair was over, the four participants never met up again. Kay returned to Wester Ross to follow her career as a schoolteacher. Now in her 80s, she resides in a care home in Altbea.

In 2008 a movie version of the story was released. *Stone of Destiny* stirred me greatly. It was unusual to see a film from a purely Scottish standpoint with no sense of Scottish 'cringe', and it followed the true story of the events to a T. Kate Mara plays Kay Matheson. For anyone wanting to know the details of what transpired in 1950, it does a damn good job.

I was raised with my mother, who recalled these events well and told me of the audacious raid by the four young Scots. By the time I started school, the talisman that is the Stone of Destiny was well known to me. I was a teenager before I travelled to London to see it for myself, where it lay behind an iron fence in Westminster Abbey. I reached through the bars to try and touch it, this lump of sandstone that had meant so much to my forebears. But it was tantalisingly out of the reach of my fingertips. As a Scot, just touching it meant so much.

As someone who moves in Scottish patriot circles, my path has crossed that of Ian Hamilton. He has spoken at Wallace Day in Elderslie and, of course, I was a member of the organising committee. On another occasion, while attending an author event in Vancouver, Canada, I was asked to talk to the local Burns club. A gentleman introduced himself afterwards. It was none other than Gavin Vernon, who had emigrated to Canada in 1962. This was a delight to me: my boyhood bedtime stories actually becoming a reality. Gavin died in March 2004 and I read of his death with great sadness. Alan Stuart has taken very much a back seat since those events, keeping well out of the limelight.

I have never met Kay Matheson, but hers is a name I hold in high regard. Young Scots, myself included, were raised on the story of the taking of the Stone. Kay showed the people of Scotland that ordinary folk could make a difference if they had the grit to get up there and do so.

To see a connection with Kay, it makes sense to say that you should go and see the Stone of Destiny sitting amidst the Crown Jewels in Edinburgh Castle – it was eventually returned to Scotland in 1996, 700 years after Edward I took it south. I travelled to the border to watch it cross over the River Tweed back to its homeland. Stories abound as to whether this is the 'real' Stone, but Ian Hamilton says that it is indeed the one that they slid out of the Coronation Chair, the one that was returned down south from Arbroath Abbey. You can see the crack where it was repaired.

As I have mentioned in an earlier chapter, the old legends say that wherever the Stone is kept, from there the Scots shall be ruled. Within a year of the Stone returning from London, Scots voted for their own parliament to reconvene, and that means the Scots are governed from Edinburgh where the Stone is kept. Some of our oldest legends still have real meaning.

Epilogue

THINGS ARE CHANGING in Scotland, and I don't just mean on the political front. There is a new awareness inherent in the people, an awareness of being Scottish. In my own lifetime I have seen the made-up 'nation' of Britain fade, although our whole education system was geared to instil Britishness upon us, and Scotland and Scottishness has once again come to the fore.

Where the Union Flag of Empire once flew, the ancient Saltire of Scotland, the white cross of St Andrew in the blue summer's sky, flies again in its rightful place.

Women played a big part in catalysing these changes. The political climate started to alter in 1967 when Winnie Ewing won a seat in Hamilton for the Scottish National Party and put the wheels in motion that would result in the people voting to reconvene Scotland's parliament. Winnie suffered sexist and derogatory abuse at the beginning of her career, but she overcame it, standing firm, knowing she had to do her best for her country. Eventually she became known as 'Madame Écosse' in the European Parliament. I met her once at Wallace Day in Elderslie. Graciously, when asked, she said a few words to the assembled throng.

Another political stalwart of the late 20th century was Margo MacDonald, who, like Winnie, proved her sexist detractors wrong and is now written into the political stonework of Scotland.

Another aspect of this reinvigoration of Scottish nationhood has been a real upsurge in artisans making Scottish products such as Scottish weaponry – swords, targes, dirks etc – and leather bags and sporrans embossed with Celtic symbols. Kilt-makers have never been busier. I don't think any male in Scotland would dare to get married in anything other than a kilt! Most Scots now seem to own one. It's hard to spot a male at a football or rugby international who is not wearing one. Women too wear more and more tartan, announcing who and what they are.

My friend Christine MacLeod is the curator at the Weavers Cottage at Kilbarchan, a National Trust for Scotland property. Christine has many of the 'old' skills when it comes to the world of weaving. She created the plaid I wore for the Wallace commemorations in August 2005, to mark the seven centuries since Wallace was murdered at London's Smithfield after his sham trial at Westminster Hall. Christine picked the plants to create the dyes, she spun the wool and she wove the life-story of Wallace into the fabric; there were 700 strands of the russet in the pattern, one line for each of the years since Wallace died. It took her three months to create it all by hand, no differently from the old tartans of Scotland, with no electricity used!

Christine is one of those who prides herself in her Scottishness and this pride is woven into her work. Every piece that she makes is unique, expressing her deep sense of how it should be comprised, so that it becomes other than just the pattern and more of a tangible embodiment of what it represents.

I can't finish this book without mentioning Elspeth King. Elspeth has been the curator at Glasgow's People's Palace, at the Abbot House in Dunfermline, and is currently at the Stirling Smith Art Gallery and Museum. Everywhere she has worked she has increased visitor numbers many-fold. She has a knack of finding the artefacts to put on show that not only embody Scotland but are what people want to see.

Elspeth was the catalyst that began my writing career. Back in the 1990s I attended a talk she gave in which she mentioned the amount of Wallace-related places in Scotland's landscape, adding: 'Wouldn't it be brilliant if someday, someone listed them.' Hence my first book, *On the Trail of William Wallace*.

She has a genius for putting people together too, and many of the folk I have worked with over the years I have met through something that Elspeth did. Just a show, a wee event, but subconsciously she seems to create links, and I have met some wonderful and talented people through her. She writes too, and has long been a champion of the almost forgotten stories of the women of Scotland, and has had a hand in creating memorials to many of them.

What I am really trying to say is that there are women out there, proud of their inheritance, proud of what they are and where they came from, and the future of Scotland is safe in their hands. Scotland is arguably the oldest nation-state on the planet and half of those proud to call themselves Scots over the centuries have been of the fairer sex. They have strived long and hard to reach a state of equality.

We have a future where we can all – Scots men and women – pull our weight together.

For Scotland. As it was. As it is. As it always will be.

James the Good: The Black Douglas

David R. Ross

ISBN 1 906307 34 2 PBK £9.99

James of Douglas rode into battle with Robert the Bruce, nearly captured Edward II after Bannockburn and chased the English out of the Borders. Known as the Good Sir James by the Scots, and the Black Douglas by the English, he was a great warrior in the Scottish Wars of Independence, yet is barely known in his own country today.

700 years ago, all Scottish castles and strongholds were in the hands of the English. James played an integral role in reinstating Scotland as an independent nation, and his is an incredible story by any standards. James was a brilliant tactician and champion. He retook Douglas Castle from English forces in such a fearsome manner that it became known as Castle Dangerous, laid siege to Carlisle, and as Warden of the Marches, raided deep into northern England. After the Bruce's death, James took the king's heart on crusade in Spain, where he met his end fighting for the Christian army.

David R. Ross reconstructs the battles that James fought in, explains how the greatly-outnumbered Scots managed to win the day at Bannockburn, and provides maps of the places where James fought and visited in Scotland, England and Spain. He has uncovered new evidence that explains many things previously unknown about the life of the remarkable 'Black Douglas'.

Desire Lines: A Scottish Odyssey

David R. Ross

ISBN 1 906307 36 9 PBK £12.99

A must read for every Scot, everyone living in Scotland and everyone visiting Scotland!

David R. Ross not only shows us his Scotland but he teaches us it too. You feel as though you are on the back of his motorcycle listening to the stories of his land as you fly with him up and down the smaller roads, the 'desire lines', of Scotland. Ross takes us off the beaten track and away from the main routes chosen for us by modern road builders.

He starts our journey in England and criss-crosses the border telling the bloody tales of the towns and villages. His recounting of Scottish history, its mythsand its legends is unapologetically and unashamedly pro-Scots.

Pride and passion for his country, the people, the future of Scotland; and his uncompromising patriotism shines through *Desire Lines*, Ross's homage to his beloved country.

David Ross is a passionate patriot. He is not afraid of stating his opinion, and he does so with unabashed gusto. The result is an enlightening travel book. But beware, it may tempt you on to a motorbike... SCOTS MAGAZINE

On the Trail of Scotland's History

David R. Ross

ISBN 1 905222 85 8 PBK £7.99

Popular historian David R. Ross tracks Scotland through the ages, detailing incidents, places and people that are key to Scotland's history, from the Dark Ages to Devolution. Leading his readers to ancient monuments and the stories surrounding them, to modern cities and the burial sites of kings, Ross guides us on a quest to discover the essentials of Scottish history – and to find things we never knew existed.

From William Wallace's possible steps, the legend of King Arthur and the reign of Robert the Bruce, to rugged raging battlegrounds, moors and mountains, and Scottish film locations, Ross's journey around Scotland links the past to the present, bringing us face-to-face with the elements that have created the Scotland of today. An essential read for those who are passionate about Scotland and its mysterious and beautiful tapestry of history and landscape.

The biker-historian's unique combination of unabashed romanticism and easy irreverence make him the ideal guide to historical subjects all too easily swallowed up in maudlin sentiment or 'demythologized' by the academic studies. THE SCOTSMAN

... an entertainingly outspoken companion for any inquisitive traveller round this nation. THE HERALD

On the Trail of Robert the Bruce

David R. Ross

ISBN 0 946487 52 9 PBK £7.99

Scots historian David R. Ross charts the story of Scotland's hero-king from his boyhood, through his days of indecision as Scotland suffered under the English yoke, to his assumption of the crown exactly six months after the death of William Wallace.

Here is the astonishing blow by blow account of how, against fearful odds, Bruce led the Scots to win their greatest ever victory. Bannockburn was not the end of the story. The war against English oppression lasted another 14 years. Bruce lived just long enough to see his dreams of an independent Scotland come to fruition in 1328 with the signing of the Treaty of Edinburgh.

The trail takes us to Bruce sites in Scotland, many of the little known and forgotten battle sites in northern England, and as far afield as the Bruce monuments in Andalusia and Jerusalem.

On the Trail of Robert the Bruce is not all blood and gore. It brings out the love and laughter, pain and passion of one of the great eras of Scottish history. Read it and you will understand why David R. Ross has never knowingly killed a spider in his life.

On the Trail of William Wallace

David R. Ross

ISBN 0 946487 47 2 PBK £7.99

On the Trail of William Wallace offers a refreshing insight into the life and heritage of the great Scots hero whose proud story is at the very heart of what it means to be Scottish, and whose effect on the ordinary Scot through the ages is manifest in the many sites where his memory is marked.

In trying to piece together the jigsaw of the reality of William Wallace's life, *On the Trail of William Wallace* weaves a subtle flow of new information with Ross's own observations. His engaging, thoughtful and at times amusing narrative reads with the ease of a historical novel, complete with all the intrigue, treachery and romance required to hold the attention of the casual reader and still entice the more knowledgeable historian.

On the Trail of William Wallace will be enjoyed by anyone with an interest in Scotland, from the passing tourist to the most fervent nationalist. It is an encyclopedia-cum-guide book, literally stuffed with fascinating titbits not usuallyon offer in the conventional history books.

The biker-historian's unique combination of unabashed romanticism and easy irreverence make him the ideal guide to historical subjects. THE SCOTSMAN

On the Trail of Bonnie Prince Charlie

David R. Ross

ISBN 0 946487 68 5 PBK £7.99

On the Trail of Bonnie Prince Charlie is the story of the Young Pretender. Born in Italy, grandson of James VII, at a time when the German house of Hanover was on the throne, his father was regarded by many as the rightful king. Bonnie Prince Charlie's campaign to retake the throne in his father's name changed the fate of Scotland. The suffering following the battle of Culloden in 1746 still evokes emotion. Charles' own journey immediately after Culloden is well known: hiding in the heather, escaping to Skye with Flora MacDonald. Little is known of his return to London in 1750 incognito, where he converted to Protestantism (he reconverted to Catholicism before he died and is buried in the Vatican). He was often unwelcome in Europe after the failure of the uprising and came to hate any mention of Scotland and his lost chance.

Yet again popular historian David R. Ross brings his own style to one of Scotland's most famous figures. Bonnie Prince Charlie is part of the folklore of Scotland. He brings forth feelings of antagonism from some and romanticism from others, but all agree on his legal right to the throne.

Ross writes with an immediacy, a dynamism, that makes his subjects come alive on the page. DUNDEE COURIER

on for Scotland

Ross

2 019 2 PBK £5.99

This is not a history book.
But it covers history.
This is not a travel guide.
But some places mentioned might be worth a visit.
This is not a political manifesto.
But a personal one.

Read this book. It might make you angry. It might give you hope. You might shed a tear. You might not agree with David R. Ross. But read this book. You might rediscover your roots, your passion for Scotland.

David R. Ross is passionate about Scotland's past, and its future. In this heartfelt journey through Scotland's story, he shares his passion for what it means to be a Scot, tackling the Act of Union, the Jacobite rebellion and revealing, for the first time, the final resting places of all Scotland's Kings and Queens.

A Passion for Scotland *sounds a clarion call to Scots worldwide to revive genuine patriotism.*
SCOTTISH TOURIST GUIDE

For Freedom: The Last Days of William Wallace

David R. Ross

ISBN 1 905222 28 9 PBK £7.99

David R. Ross, the 'biker-historian', goes on the trail of William Wallace again to investigate his last days, the events that led up to his death, and their repercussions through Scottish history. He ties Wallace's life and death to the issues of patriotism and Scottish nationality over the last 700 years and identifies Wallace as a 'Scottish Martyr' who died for freedom and identity in the country he loved.

Luath Press Limited

committed to publishing well written books worth read

LUATH PRESS takes its name from Robert Burns, whose little collie Luath (*Gael.*, swift or nimble) tripped up Jean Armour at a wedding and gave him the chance to speak to the woman who was to be his wife and the abiding love of his life. Burns called one of the 'Twa Dogs' Luath after Cuchullin's hunting dog in Ossian's *Fingal*.

Luath Press was established in 1981 in the heart of Burns country, and is now based a few steps up the road from Burns' first lodgings on Edinburgh's Royal Mile. Luath offers you distinctive writing with a hint of unexpected pleasures.

Most bookshops in the UK, the US, Canada, Australia, New Zealand and parts of Europe, either carry our books in stock or can order them for you. To order direct from us, please send a £sterling cheque, postal order, international money order or your credit card details (number, address of cardholder and expiry date) to us at the address below. Please add post and packing as follows: UK – £1.00 per delivery address; overseas surface mail – £2.50 per delivery address; overseas airmail – £3.50 for the first book to each delivery address, plus £1.00 for each additional book by airmail to the same address. If your order is a gift, we will happily enclose your card or message at no extra charge.

Luath Press Limited

543/2 Castlehill
The Royal Mile
Edinburgh EH1 2ND
Scotland
Telephone: +44 (0)131 225 4326 (24 hours)
Fax: +44 (0)131 225 4324
email: sales@luath. co.uk
Website: www. luath.co.uk